NATIONALISATION

BEYOND THE SLOGANS

NATIONALISATION

BEYOND THE SLOGANS

KEITH COLEMAN

RAVAN PRESS
Johannesburg

Published by Ravan Press Pty (Ltd)
3rd Floor, Standard House, 40 de Korte Street, Braamfontein
PO Box 31134, Braamfontein 2017, South Africa

First published 1991

ISBN 0 86975 413 0

DTP setting by Ravan Press

Printed by Clyson Printers, Cape Town

FOR LAUREN

ACKNOWLEDGEMENTS

Numerous people have helped, coaxed and coerced me in the course of writing this book. Thanks to Nic and Mark, who made me run the gauntlet when I submitted a longer, less readable version of this book to the Wits Business School as part of my Masters in Business Administration. Many thanks go to my editor, John Carlin, who, when the going got slow, got tough. To Sue, for the cover. And to Glen, Ingrid and the Ravan staff who got it all together in record time.

WE need to move beyond slogans. This book is a step in that direction. It shows that nationalisation is a workable instrument, which can play an important role in redistribution and economic planning. As South Africans we have often been extremely parochial and self-absorbed. the author provides useful international comparative material on success stories as well as failures of nationalisation. This book shows the limitations of nationalisation under the control of a top-heavy, central state bureaucracy. It reveals alternatives which opens up the possibility of greater public, democratic control which could be food for thought for the South African Communist Party, and indeed should be for other South Africans too.

Joe Slovo, general secretary, South African Communist Party

SOME may argue that nationalisation is a defective strategy addressing a real problem, namely structural inequality in the economy. Others think by pointing out the defects in the strategy the problem need not be addressed. Coleman makes a timely and refreshing contribution to a debate more often obscured by dogmatism and hot air than rational discussion. His eye remains unerringly on the central problem of structural inequality, particularly in South Africa.

Frederick van Zyl Slabbert, director of the Institute for Democratic Alternatives in South Africa.

THE question of nationalising private business is a highly emotive subject that has, in the light of the recent changes in South Africa's political landscape, been the focus of much debate. Many of the arguments put forward thus far both in support of or against nationalisation have tended to be subjective and devoid of sound comprehensive reasoning. The analytical approach by the author of this book provides the reader with a clear understanding of the principle motives behind the rationale of those who advocate nationalisation. It also provides well researched and interesting case studies of nationalisation that has occurred around the world over the last 60 years. While I personally have considerable problems with the concept of nationalisation I must compliment the author on his dispassionate review of the wide range of factors that come into play in considering whether government should take over private enterprise. As he explores the subject in more detail a diverse range of influences and processes that affect all forms of nationalisation unfold. The text enables an holistic view to be formed as it examines the issue from both an internal perspective, ie the interests of the employees, and from an external perspective, ie the relationship to market-driven forces. On the question of incentives however, the inarguable imperative for improving productivity is not really addressed and this crucial aspect will have to be analysed further in the debate. The publication of this book is timely and will make an extremely useful contribution to the discussion on nationalisation at a time in South Africa's history when events and changes in attitudes are moving rapidly.

Ken Maxwell, past-president of the Chamber of Mines and currently a director of JCI.

CONTENTS

APPENDIX 3

LIST OF TABLES

INTRODUCTION

Politicians of all shades have advocated nationalisation — communists, socialists, social democrats, liberals, conservatives, fascists. Stalin nationalised, and so did Mussolini, Attlee, Roosevelt, Edward Heath.

In fact every country has done it: South Africa, Yemen, Sweden, Germany and the United States. It has failed in Eastern Europe, Zambia and Ethiopia. It has worked in Mexico, Norway and South Korea. It has been imposed from above. It has been negotiated. Owners of business have requested it.

And, no, the communists did not invent it. It predates them by several thousand years. It was used in Ancient Babylon, Greece and Rome, by the Hanseatic League of Northern Germany in the Middle Ages, during colonial expansion, and to modernise Japan.

Nationalisation has been done in peace and war, boom and slump, depressions, recessions, reconstructions and economic miracles.

Anyone who rejects nationalisation outright has not been to the Tennessee Valley in the United States or the oil-fields of the North Sea; has not chatted to Gavin Relly; has not understood what's been going on when taking a train, calling a policeman, flushing a toilet.

As for those who swear by nationalisation, who conceive of it as the cure to all ills, they had better go quickly to Eastern Europe, earn wages in a Zambian copper mine or find out what happened to the Peruvian iron industry.

In short, reader, suspend your doubts and prejudices. Set aside political principles and utopian ideals. For if you're not ready to strike a balance between the desirable and the possible there is no point even in starting to discuss the issue.

To pose the question 'To nationalise, or not to nationalise?' is not to descend into madness. For there is genuine promise to nationalisation. The promise of access for the poor to basic needs, of balanced growth and world competitiveness, of redistribution of wealth and the return of land to the dispossessed.

There is also room for fear — of economic decline, of inefficiency and bureaucracy, of the disappearance of the market mechanism, or of irrational allocation of resources.

Too much emotion has been invested in the 'N-Word'. Nelson Mandela got the ball rolling just after his release from prison. He was labelled 'naive' and 'out of touch' for suggesting the nationalisation of banks, mines and monopolies. Too much politics, the critics bayed, too little economics, too much principle, too little strategy.

The pro-nationalisers and anti-nationalisers formed into camps and then they built fortresses around themselves. On the one side the African National Congress, the Congress of South African Trade Unions, the South African Communist Party were joined by a variety of socialists advocating collective ownership of the means of production and by African nationalists seeking the return of wealth to those they deemed to be its rightful owners.

Across the no-man's-land businessmen and government officials watched warily. There, behind their high walls, they stood: the free-marketeer capitalists who associate economic growth and prosperity with individual effort and profit, with privatisation and deregulation.

Yes, the protagonists in the two camps did talk, but past one another. No common understanding was reached even of the definition of the word nationalisation. For nationalisation has meant different things to different people. One man's confiscation, it has been found, is another man's redistribution.

In those moments when the debate has deviated into reason, those against have based their arguments on the principle that what is good for the individual company is good for the whole economy, and those for have argued that what is good for the country is good for everyone.

That first battle in February 1990 raised so much dust that reason, by and large, was blinded. ANC supporters cheered Mandela's support for nationalisation. And business was dismayed, the market value of the Johannesburg Stock Exchange falling by R38-billion — having gained R28-billion after De Klerk's speech two weeks earlier announcing Mandela's imminent release.

Mandela did not understand the 'hullabaloo'. He called it 'totally misconceived because nationalisation of certain sectors of the economy is part of the history of this country.'[1]

And he was not wrong. Nationalisation is indeed an established part of South Africa's economic history.

State involvement in the economy was already firmly established in the 1920s. 'Long before the postwar nationalisations in the West, South Africa had placed all its major utilities and several of its industries under national ownership.'[2] Many of these public companies were established from scratch — like the South African Post Office, with interests in postal services, telecommunications and banking services, even marketing boards.

There were three main reasons for these nationalisations:

● To develop industries not prioritised by private capital, but essential to the development of an advanced economy. Such as the Iron and Steel Corporation (Iscor, now privatised). Like South African Transport Services, with a monopoly over railways, dominance in air transport, and interests in road transport. Also Eskom, which supplies all electricity.

● As a strategic response to oil and arms embargoes imposed against apartheid. The state set out to make South Africa self-sufficient in arms and munitions through Armscor (but failed). And in energy through Sasol (and failed again).

● Successive governments, particularly after 1948, sought to provide whites with a high standard of living. Apartheid governments nationalised and regulated where their ideological aims were not achieved by the private sector alone. Preferential jobs were given to whites within the expanding state sector. Services were provided to white Group Areas, while few services were provided in black areas.

In 1943, National Party leader DF Malan proposed that the state intervene to 'the maximum possible degree in the economy to help the Afrikaner achieve his rightful share' of South Africa's economic cake.[3] He proposed to nationalise Anglo American, which dominated the mining industry. In self-defence Anglo assisted Barlows, an industrial conglomerate, to take over Rand Mines, an ailing mining company; and in the 1960s Federale Mynbou to take over General Mining.

Nationalisation was part of state economic policy for the four decades of National Party rule. By 1960 the public sector's share of gross domestic product was 23%. By 1975 it was 30%. In 1980 the state-owned enterprises employed 34% of economically active whites and about 16% of other groups. Eskom alone accounted for over 40% of spending on new plant and machinery. Today the state sector accounts for about 40% of the country's assets and about 40% of GDP.

Recently government economic policy has shifted to privatising state assets and decreasing direct state involvement in the economy. This, while the Mass Democratic Movement has begun emphasising the economic aims of the Freedom Charter, which considers nationalising another 40% (or so) of the economy.

Which is another reason why there has been so much heat, and so little light, in the South African debate. The issue has been plagued by false dichotomies, by the notion that nationalisation and privatisation, central planning and the free market, are mutually exclusive. But there is no reason why there cannot be privatisation and nationalisation at the same time. Or both planning and market forces within the same economic programme.

There is nothing inherently capitalist or right wing about privatisation. That allegation should be directed at the context in which it is done, the programme into which it fits. The same with nationalisation. It is not inherently socialist. Privatisation is not proof nationalisation does not work. Neither is the reverse true.

The same with central planning and the market. For many years social ownership and central planning gave the Soviet economy immense impetus. Then stagnation set in. A country once closing in on the world's advanced nations saw the gap widen again — in efficiency, quality, science and technology. The decline called into question the wisdom of central planning and nationalisation, and the efficiency and effectiveness of centrally-planned versus market economies.

Some crudely say the collapse of Eastern European and the Soviet economy vindicates the untrammeled market, open competition and the profit-motive to the exclusion of all else. But a distinction must be drawn between a centrally-planned and a command economy. Both types of economy incorporate nationalisation, yet operate according to very different impulses. The command economy involves top-down orders for production based on a centrally-planned production schedule. Central planning allows private and nationalised industries to respond to market forces, while maintaining an overall economic scheme.

The market provides signals, incentives. It stimulates cost reduction and adaptation to technological change. Alone it cannot direct an economy. It does not show the 'optimal growth path or automatically generate socially attractive institutions.' Some needs are not market based: education, health, welfare, street lighting, urban public transport, sewers.[4]

Questions are begged: What is the relationship between planning and the market? How much planning and how much market? Can there be market socialism?

In seeking answers the old debates and false dichotomies must be cleared away, the emotions cooled. And then there will be surprises. For there are areas of common ground! Both camps agree to a mixed economy. Both want different forms of property and the involvement of the central government in economic life. Both want the market to play an important role. Both want economic growth. Most agree that nationalisation is appropriate for certain services. Management is even considering the idea that the state and workers become involved in businesses up to board level. Participative management is appealing to many.

Some of the people in favour, besides, are as critical of nationalisation as those against. Both sides, for example, object to total state ownership of everything. Both dislike the inefficiencies of command economics, fear bureaucratic tampering by politicians, warn of the dangers of state monopolies.

And once the dust has settled, the debate must start all over again. A return to basics. To the essential questions.

- Why nationalise? What does one hope to gain?

- What exactly does one want to nationalise? How will one choose?
- How will one nationalise? By what process?
- What will one do with the company once nationalised?
- Is nationalisation, indeed, feasible at all?

In seeking to answer these questions, this book will attempt first to identify what nationalisation entails — what the word actually means — and then, hopefully, lay a basis for a more rational, clear-headed debate on where, indeed whether, it should be applied as policy in South Africa.

NOTES

1. *Weekly Mail*, 16/2/90.
2. Merton Dagut, quoted in Yudelman, D, *The Emergence of Modern South Africa: State, Capital, and the Incorporation of Organized Labour on the South African Gold fields, 1902 - 1939*, David Philip, Cape Town, 1984, p281.
3. Merton Dagut, quoted in Yudelman, D, *The Emergence of Modern South Africa*, p279.
4. Cassim, F, 'The ANC's Constitutional Guidelines: An Economic Assessment'. Paper presented to The Conference on Economic Alternatives for South Africa, hosted by The Economic Society of South Africa and Wits Business School, Johannesburg, 1989, p6.

CHAPTER ONE

WHY NATIONALISE?

Before any government begins to nationalise, it must have clear reasons for doing so. This may be an obvious statement, but with the nationalisation debate still in its infancy in South Africa it needs to be said. And the broader and more imprecise the aims, the less likely nationalisation is to succeed.

But the fact remains that many good, practical and feasible reasons to nationalise have been advanced both in South Africa and elsewhere. For the ANC and Cosatu to have declared that 'nationalisation would be an essential part of the reconstruction programme of (a democratic) state'[1] is not fundamentally laughable, as some no doubt will argue.

However, the frequently wide differences between the stated aims of nationalisation in South Africa and in other countries indicates a need for the advocates of nationalisation here to think again, to return to the drawing board. Economic and social objectives, one finds, have been sacrificed at the altars of politics and ideology.

Arguments elsewhere in the world have put together coherent, if contentious, reasons to nationalise. In South Africa, however, no wholly logical, rigorous motivation has yet been put forward. This is revealed in what follows.

Part One looks at the reasons for nationalisation advanced elsewhere in the world. Part Two attempts to draw together the somewhat disparate reasons advanced as to why there should be nationalisation in South Africa. Part Three assesses the motivations for nationalisation in South Africa.

PART ONE

The aims of nationalisation elsewhere in the world

POLITICS AND IDEOLOGY

Nationalisation is usually associated with social change — a transition to socialism, to state capitalism, to a mixed economy, or within colonial situations to domestic ownership by the private sector of a broader share of productive units. The classic socialist position on nationalisation was put by Lenin:

> The struggle of the working class against the capitalist class ... can only end in the passage of political power into the hands of the working class, the transfer of all the land, instruments, factories, machines and mines to the whole of society for the organisation of socialist production.[2]

Lenin's assumption was that nationalisation would replace conflict and competition with co-operation. In the daily functioning of the nationalised enterprise, democracy would be established in the workplace, overcoming the alienation of workers from the product of their labour. The aim was to change the social relations of production within production, to change the way people work, the conditions in which they work, the status of different segments of the working class, unskilled as well as skilled, women and men, black and white; and the divisions between mental and manual labour. All this made social ownership a necessity.

Variations of classical socialism have recently emerged, led by Gorbachev and his *perestroika*, and following the collapse of the Eastern European economies. 'New socialism' distinguishes between central planning and command economies, both of which are based upon nationalised industry, but which operate according to different impulses. While the top-heavy state planning of the command economy is characterised by top-down orders for production, central planning allows greater flexibility for nationalised industries to respond to market forces, while always sticking to an overall economic plan.

Many advocates of mixed economies also support nationalisation. Many in favour of the capitalist system, but disturbed by capitalism's inability to maintain stable growth and provide security and welfare for the population, advocate nationalisation and central planning to a limited extent. They argue that the state should run essential services like health and transport in the interests of consumers, and should protect the population at large from the devastating consequences of economic failure and malpractice. Such reasoning is also driven by the desire to protect workers from poor working conditions and low rates of pay. This, in fact, was the motivation behind much of the nationalisation in Britain.

There are also those who pursue a mixed economy in search of a successful marriage between the best of socialism and the best of capitalism. These are found most often in the Third World, where distorted growth has created one or two particularly powerful economic sectors in the economy, run as monopolies. This hinders the rest of the economy, which remains underdeveloped. In such circumstances the idea of nationalising the 'commanding heights' of the economy is often posed, the goal being to give the government real control over this part of the country's economy. The rest of the economy, on this argument, should be left to individual entrepreneurs responding to market forces.

By 1990, both the ANC and the South African government advocated a mixed economy. Each perceived the term very differently. 'The existing system is a mixed economy oriented towards capitalism and ... the ANC's strategy is to build a mixed economy oriented towards socialism.'[3]

Nationalisation, public ownership and state intervention may be necessary means for socialist ends but, it becomes clear, such means may also be employed for capitalist ends. They are not instruments exclusive to the socialist domain.

Nationalisations have been carried out in the 'public interest' by pro-capitalist governments as well. In Britain there is a strong tradition which argues that some industries are healthier as public corporations, where the government takes decisions over key industries upon which the whole population is dependent. The National Health Service is the best-known example; others are the army and police services, the armament and nuclear industries. (Less well known is the fact that Lloyd George nationalised the pubs of Carlisle in 1919 to prevent the overselling of drink[4])! The aim of such control in Britain is to ensure variety of production; the quality of products; or to guarantee a service to those who cannot otherwise afford it.

In Third World economies, the central aim of nationalisation has been to achieve self-determination and economic independence. And many foreign companies have ended up nationalised in peripheral economies in the Third World's search for sovereignty over national resources. This pattern has emerged in the bulk of nationalisations over the last 60 years.

When nationalisation is motivated by the quest for self-determination, the aims are to acquire a larger share of resources (profits or foreign exchange), to achieve a greater degree of control over decision making (output and investment levels, pricing, purchase of local inputs, expansion into export markets) and to stop decapitalisation of the local economy through repatriation of profits. The rationale is that nationalising would also help develop a balanced economy. Foreign investment frequently formed an enclave within the local economy, which caused resentment and led to a structure of dual economy — 'a small, affluent, self-contained economy built around the foreign enterprise...while the balance of the economy remains in a backward state.'[5]

However, the impulse behind nationalisation has sometimes not been rationalised at all. Sometimes revenge, pure and simple, has provided the initial spark, particularly where the multinational in question has been perceived to be severely exploitative or aggressive.

ECONOMIC REASONING

Nationalisation programmes usually stress the need for a more equitable distribution of wealth. Trade unions advocating nationalisation may be aiming for better wage levels and working conditions, wishing to reclaim for the direct producers the profit otherwise appropriated by the capitalists.

A broader aim may be to directly affect the personal distribution of real incomes through, for example, reducing prices of goods bought mainly by lower income earners. The emphasis is often on basic necessities for everyone, not just those who can afford, for example, medical treatment, primary and secondary education, sometimes even universities, opera houses and museums.

Nationalisation may also prevent the changes in population distribution that may result from differential costs of living for urban and rural areas — it costs different amounts to provide the same services to people in different parts of the country. Private industry would differentiate prices on this basis, charging higher prices to match the cost of provision, but often to those who can least afford it. By nationalising gas, electricity, communications and transport, it could be possible to cross-subsidise and hold down prices.

Correcting failures of the market mechanism

Nationalisation has been advocated as a response to areas where the market mechanism is dysfunctional. The market may impose short-term constraints on projects which only have long-term competitiveness or benefits (like education and training). As such it will favour money capital over and against industrial capital; and may fail to register social costs that are real costs to capital as a whole.

Examples of the latter might include the negative cost of pollution or city congestion, or the positive gain of collective benefits such as a trained workforce.

Nationalisation aims to prevent the abuse of monopoly power where a single enterprise (a 'natural monopoly') is seen as the most efficient size of unit. 'Where a natural monopoly arises in an industry which is essential for the welfare of the community, there is always a risk that private owners may exploit their position.'[6]

Nationalisation can be used to implement restructuring where structural efficiencies are not attained. It has been argued that under private ownership an industry 'may never adopt a structure which is economically efficient ... and even where owners perceive the necessity for amalgamation, they may be unwilling to (do so).'[7]

Nationalisation may be needed to provide services and investment which are efficient from a social cost-benefit point of view, but which would register balance sheet losses and are thus not provided by private capital.

There are occasions where the economy needs a particular industry, but the cost of developing that sector is enormous, and returns will only show after a long period. The state can operate in a longer time frame than private capital, whose investors expect a shorter-term return on investment. The state can thus undertake the investments with longer-term returns.

Nationalisation has been used to prevent the huge social and economic costs caused by economic collapses and downturns — to prevent redundancies, keep wages high, keeping employment up where the lack of viability may otherwise lead to a shutting down of the industry.

Nationalisation is also advocated to ensure macro-economic stability through direct control of key industries' expenditure; and to sustain industries which are regarded as essential but which do not meet the profit criteria of the market. This should be temporary. 'In an internationally competitive market there must be something suspicious about a company in need of permanent public aid.'[8] Some socialists believe that nationalisation could increase productivity.

> Under private ownership the workforce may be unwilling to work as hard as they potentially could because they do not share in any improvement in profitability. The process of nationalisation would overcome this difficulty since the workforce would be working for the benefit of the community at large rather than for the benefit of private shareholders.[9]

Assisting state economic planning

Many governments have been attracted by nationalisation as a powerful economic planning tool that serves to counter short-term problems in business cycles and which favours long-term developmental planning for the economy. It is easier for the government to use nationalised enterprises than private companies as instruments of policy. This was shown during the war years in Britain, when it seemed desirable for the state to control the commanding heights of the economy.

In the 50 years preceding the rash of nationalisations in Africa and Latin America in the 1940-1960 period, most raw materials were extracted, exported and processed elsewhere. This meant the full benefits were not reaped by the local economy. In peripheral mono-economies dependent upon raw material production, nationalisation has been seen as a method to gain access to further points in the value chain.

International competitiveness is vital to the success of any country in today's globalised markets. Where international competitiveness is waning, nationalisation can be attempted to redevelop it. This was successfully done in South Korea and in Japan after the Second World War.

PROTECTING STRATEGIC INTERESTS

A common aim of nationalisation is to protect the vital strategic interests of a society. For example, except in the United States, atomic power is developed under the state.

Strategic aims might also be shaped by the extent to which a country can depend on external supply, particularly during wartime. Thus steel and air transport, for example, need to be maintained on a scale which may prove economically unattractive to private companies. An example of this is the 1946 British nationalisation of civil aviation for strategic and safety reasons.

When Frelimo came to power in Mozambique in 1975 it nationalised as a deliberate policy only the health service, legal practices, education, funeral services and rented property. Despite this deliberate limitation of nationalisation, 73% of the economy was nationalised within seven years. This was a product of defensive nationalisation due to an ongoing war with what was then Rhodesia; the ex-settler ruling class which simply abandoned, asset stripped and destroyed productive property; and the implications of nationalising rented property — the banks, which depended on rents and property values more than was realised, had virtually collapsed.[10]

PART TWO

The aims of nationalisation in contemporary South Africa

POLITICAL AND IDEOLOGICAL MOTIVATIONS

The new socialists in South Africa, located mostly in the trade unions and in the South African Communist Party, argue for social ownership of the means of production and planning of the economy, but not under a centralised command economy. Rather, they argue, a more democratic form of nationalisation should be adopted, to benefit the economy through increased productivity and satisfy demands for worker participation in all aspects of economic life. Old-style nationalisation is considered a limited tool if it puts control into the hands of the state rather than the hands of workers.

Joe Slovo, general secretary of the South African Communist Party, recognises that nationalisation, by itself, is not enough to achieve the objectives of a post-apartheid economy of correcting imbalances in the control and distribution of economic resources. This is Slovo's understanding of the aims of new-style nationalisation:

> A society in which the producers have a sense of participation and not alienation from the products which they produce. From that can be born a new integrated community moving towards greater equity and egalitarianism. It is a combination of redistribution of wealth, giving the state the power to upgrade conditions for disadvantaged people, participation of workers, moving towards socialisation. It is not just based on some idealistic ideological perspective.[11]

A strong message coming out of the Congress of South African Trade Unions is that nationalisation can facilitate worker participation in key management decisions. Jay Naidoo, general secretary of Cosatu, has said:

> The juridical ownership of enterprises is ... not as crucial as the need to ensure that workers have a say in determining policies that a democratic government will take on the economy and a range of other issues affecting our membership such as housing, education, investment and job creation.[12]

Alec Erwin, education officer of the National Union of Metalworkers of South Africa (Numsa) and leading member of the SACP argues that a future socialist economy in South Africa should be a mixed economy:

> Collective ownership of one or another sort is an essential requirement although not a guarantee of worker control.' A national plan will be more effective if implemented with economic incentives where there has been 'worker participation in formulating the objectives and then in implementing the plan. This opens the way for collective ownership both as a means of planning and as a component of democracy.[13]

The ANC adds that to achieve the twin aims of redistribution and high economic growth 'the new democratic order will necessarily have to address the question of ownership, control and direction of the economy as a whole to ensure that neither the public nor private sectors serve as a means of enriching the few at the expense of the majority.'[14] Nationalisation is thus viewed as a means of restoring a degree of political equity to the economy.

At a workshop to discuss future economic policy held in Harare in April 1990, and hosted by the ANC and Cosatu the general consensus was that future economic policy would aim to transform imbalances between blacks and whites, urban and rural, and between regions.[15] Thabo Mbeki of the ANC's national executive said:

> The present economic system has been distorted by monopolies and cartels, and the system has gross inequalities and imbalances that have produced great poverty within the black sector of the population. Any democratic government will have to alter the structures inside the economy in order to create a system which can redress these imbalances. The issue is who controls the wealth in order to effect a more equitable system of distribution. Nationalisation remains an option in the restructuring of the economy.[16]

Nationalisation, the argument continues, could deconcentrate industry, removing the power base of apartheid capitalism.[17] Over 80% of all shares on the Johannesburg Stock Exchange (JSE) are controlled by four companies. In 1984 all companies quoted on the JSE were controlled by only 2 554 directors — and nearly 20% of all directorships were in the hands of just 65 men. Concentration is perceived to be bad because of price collusion, difficulty of entry for smaller corporations, and over-powerful employers bargaining with comparatively smaller unions.

Mandela has argued for dismembering, or nationalising conglomerates. 'We must look,' he said, 'at how to ensure that there is no unhealthy over-concentration of economic power.'[18]

REDISTRIBUTING WEALTH

Redistribution of incomes is the most frequently stated reason for nationalisation in South Africa, where there are vast disparities in wealth. South Africa's GINI Coefficient (an internationally-accepted standard measuring the disparity in incomes in a single country) was 0,56 in 1965. It deteriorated to 0,68 in 1975 making it a nation with one of the highest levels of inequality on earth. 'Nationalisation is the best method to ... rid South Africa of present inequalities in terms of wealth.'[19]

The trade unions aim to redistribute wealth away from the owners of industry to workers, seeking 'wealth creation with guaranteed minimum living wage levels.'[20] Redistribution, they say, will also be achieved through redistribution of services. Under the clause: 'There Shall be Houses, Security and Comfort!' The Freedom Charter states:

> A preventive health scheme shall be run by the state; free medical care and hospitalisation shall be provided for all, with special care for mothers and young children... The aged the orphans, the disabled and sick shall be cared for by the state...[21]

ANC economists have questioned the ability of the market mechanism alone to provide for economic growth and the needs of the population. The ANC's constitutional proposals do not aim to eliminate the market sector, but they do seek mechanisms to benefit those not equipped to compete in the market place. For example, Mandela has argued for the state filling investment gaps: 'We must consider whether there are no areas in which it would benefit society at large if the state established public corporations or strengthened existing ones.'[22] Housing, he suggested, might be one of these areas.

State interventions into economic management have increased since the Second World War. Nationalisation, it is felt, may be necessary for activities the private sector will not undertake because the costs of collecting revenue are too high, the recovery of the initial outlay could take too long, or the initial capital investment required is too great.

On another level, it is argued that nationalisation of industry is necessary to protect, and increase, the number of jobs. Labour supply is increasing, but employment figures have remained static over the last ten years. This is partly because conglomerates have been committed to cutting costs and decreasing employment.

Given the strength of the trade union movement in South Africa, as well as the impact it is having on the nationalisation debate, it is no surprise that one of the often-stated aims of nationalisation is changing the social relations of production.

The argument used is that the present framework of production helps shape the ideology, culture and goals to which people in society aspire. The framework of the future has to break the ideology of apartheid. Recommendations from the Harare conference in April 1990 state that the labour process in South Africa needs reorganisation along with skills training and technology. 'Collective ownership will favour employment creation and it will mediate the excessively exploitative relationships that generally develop in small individually owned enterprises as they compete for a share of the market.'[23] Martin Nicol, the National Union of Mineworkers economist, argues:

> Only a nationalised mining industry, as part of a socially planned economy, will enable workers to achieve the objectives of ... a minimum wage on all mines; the same pay for the same jobs on all mines; excellent living conditions for mineworkers; the highest standards of health and safety.[24]

The ANC aims to plan for a viable economy which will benefit the majority of South Africans. Clause 'O' of the ANC's Constitutional Guidelines gives the state 'the right to determine the general context in which economic life takes place and define and limit the rights and obligations attaching to ownership and use of productive property.'[25]

Nationalisation thus comes to be seen as an option in the economic tool kit of a future South Africa. Mbeki argues that 'South Africa's economy will need restructuring and it would be wrong to avoid considering an element of nationalisation as part of a possible solution.'[26] For the new economy must be resilient enough to adjust to changes in world markets, and forward-looking enough to reconstruct South Africa's position in the world economy.

Nationalisation could achieve this through raising the level of investment and directing that investment towards the infrastructure or towards basic consumer necessities. There could also be state corporations involved in research, development and marketing of new technology and products. These corporations could shape the product mix and pricing structures of private sector corporations by competing with them on the open market.

SELF-DETERMINATION AND THE LAND QUESTION

Earlier, it was seen that one of the chief aims of nationalisation in Third World countries was to gain sovereignty over national resources, enabling the people of that country to achieve self-determination.

This aim has expression in South Africa, but in a slightly different form. Nationalisation of 'the people's' assets would return them to the people as a whole rather than leaving them in the hands of whites only. This position is strongly advocated by the Pan Africanist Congress.

The ANC view on this is the same. It arises out of the perception that South Africa is characterised by 'internal colonialism' or 'colonialism of a special type' (CST is the acronym familiar in ANC and SACP circles) which considers South Africa a capitalist state, created and established by conquest and settlement, in which the indigenous black people are still struggling for self-determination. Part of that struggle involves returning the wealth to 'the people'. Nationalisation aims to do that.

Land redistribution is a central national grievance and raising agricultural production is vital to future economic prosperity. Proposed ANC agricultural policy would aim to:

- Return land to those removed from black freehold farms and the repossession of land by certain categories of labour tenants;
- Redistribute land and relocate people through a land commission;
- Promote smallholder, co-operative and joint ventures;
- Reallocate support services and training provisions to achieve redistribution while maintaining production;
- Redistribute land to create employment and provide secure housing.[27]

A variant of the position which sees nationalisation redressing racial imbalances argues that it will simply put things back into their rightful place. The South African Youth Congress president Peter Mokaba epitomised this position when he called for nationalisation, saying: 'I find it strange that Barend du Plessis (the government's minister of finance) labels the ANC's nationalisation policy as theft. Who are we stealing our own wealth from?'[28]

This argument is particularly strong in relation to the land. A programme of nationalisation based on the CST analysis would aim to restore wealth to the African people as a whole as distinct from redistribution or worker participation. The land becomes a crucial area where reform programmes have a distinct retributive/restorative nature. Consider the following argument:

> The principal target of land reform must be commercial agriculture... The primary economic objective will be to increase wage foods and agricultural produce in general... The same land reform will have as its target all black rural people, because black people have been discriminated against by every agrarian reform in CST conditions.[29]

Overcoming the legacy of apartheid is a fundamental issue, which will require more than the mere repeal of racial laws such as the 1913 Land Act and the Group Areas Act to achieve increased agricultural productivity and rural development.

> There is a need to articulate a policy frame for placing ownership of land in the hands of users through an agrarian reform process. Such a process will inevitably include expropriation, nationalisation and negotiation as a means of land redistribution.[30]

The case for 'nationalisation to achieve equity' can most easily be made for labour tenant and black spot land. The land would be restored to the previously removed community or to the occupying labour tenants.

There is a proposal from some opposition groups to nationalise land presently occupied by whites, to return it to blacks from whom it was originally taken. This will encompass 'all black rural people, because black people have been discriminated against by every agrarian reform in CST conditions.'[31] Thus land should be restored through reversing the process of colonial conquest.

Industry, on the other hand, developed more recently. The industries, mines and banks were not part of an actual dispossession process. Thus, it is not those means of production which are being returned, but the fruits of their production. There are not competing claims to ownership of the resource; simply argument about how they should best be used. Nationalisation is seen as necessary to deconcentrate industry, removing the power base of apartheid capitalism. It is also seen as a mechanism to overcome racial privilege and injustice through, among others, redistribution of wealth, services and power. There would be no seizure of assets from one group to give to another — nationalisation would involve aims of democratisation, worker control and state intervention.

Industrial nationalisation then is not clothed in moral or historical arguments; and there is no motivation for revenge or compensating past ills. It is simply a forward-looking 'what is best for the future?' approach. This dichotomy in nationalisation's aims is introduced by the CST analysis, particularly in the case of land nationalisation. But the target of land nationalisation becomes unclear — is it the white farmer, or agribusiness or just those who occupied land vacated by black-spot removals? So far there are competing proposals: labour tenants would have their land restored; black spot land would be restored to the previously removed community; victims of forced removals would get their land back.

There are fewer suggestions for socialisation of the farms, as opposed to industry. But agribusiness and even owner-farmers could be treated the same way as manufacturing — which strengthens the argument for socialisation, participation and worker control rather than restoring to the people.

Thus there is a tension in the aims of land nationalisation. The idea lacks the clarity of intent evident when other parts of the economy are discussed. Perhaps this is because of the restoring consequences of the CST analysis. However, there need not be a contradiction between the different aims. It is possible to have restoring aims for certain categories of land (such as black spots and victims of removals), while at the same time having socialisation aims for agribusiness. The question still remains: how far back does the restoring aim go? The 1960-1990 period of black-spot dispossession, or the 1913 Land Act dispossession, or even further back to the original wars of conquest?

PART THREE

Assessing the aims of nationalisation

While it is logical that the aims of nationalisation in South Africa would differ from those elsewhere, there are some notable omissions, as outlined in Table 1.

Certain categories — such as transforming control into ownership — have emerged due to peculiar features in other countries, and need not be raised in South Africa. There are others, such as socialising commodities, welfare optimisation, and to a lesser extent 'natural monopolies', which are arguably incorporated within other aims. However, certain key aims — such as structural efficiencies, response to economic crisis, economies of scale, developing the value chain, overcoming inefficiencies and responding to international developments in an industry — are not mentioned at all.

By the same token, the aims for South African nationalisation which have not been a factor elsewhere are to correct racial imbalances; and re-nationalisation.

The following received far more emphasis in South Africa than elsewhere: control over monopoly power; redistribution, particularly from white to black; industrial democracy, accountability to workers and socialisation.

TABLE 1: A comparative analysis of the aims of nationalisation in South Africa and the rest of the world

Aims of nationalisation	Included in SA	Source
Ideological		
Classical socialism	No	
The new socialism	Yes	SACP, Cosatu, academics
Mixed economies	Yes	ANC, academics
Political		
Industrial democracy	Yes	Cosatu, SACP
Shifting decision making to a group responsible to the public	Yes	ANC, academics
To achieve national self-determination	Yes	ANC
Economic		
Redistribution of wealth (incomes)	Yes	ANC, Cosatu, SACP, academics
Redistribution of wealth (services)	Yes	ANC, Cosatu, SACP, academics
To socialise commodities	No	
Correcting failures of the market mechanism	Yes	ANC, academics
'Natural monopolies'	No	
Structural efficiencies	No	
Filling an investment gap	Yes	ANC, Cosatu, academics
Preserving/ creating employment	Yes	ANC, Cosatu
Response to economic or profitability crisis	No	
Cost-benefit optimisation	No	
Economies of scale	No	
Increasing productivity	Yes	Cosatu
Developing the value chain	No	
Changing employment practices	Yes	Cosatu
As a response to international developments in the industry	No	
To assist economic planning by the state	Yes	ANC, Cosatu
Overcoming inefficiencies at national level	No	
Stabilising and macro-economic objectives	Yes	Academics
Transforming control into ownership	No	
Other		
Strategic and safety	No	
Defensive	No	
Included in SA but not elsewhere		
Correcting racial imbalances		ANC, Cosatu, SACP, academics
Control over monopoly power		ANC, Cosatu, SACP
Re-nationalisation		ANC, Cosatu, SACP
Restoring the Land to its rightful owners		ANC, Cosatu, SACP

Too much politics

The stated objectives of nationalisation in South Africa emphasise achieving political democracy (at different levels); developing society's control mechanisms to produce and allocate wealth in a non-racial fashion; redressing historical racial imbalances in distribution and ownership of wealth; and challenging existing economic power structures. The context in which these objectives are put forward is highly politicised. Put simply, nationalisation is seen as an antidote to apartheid.

In Britain, the balance was reversed: nationalisation was aimed at achieving primarily economic ends — to correct imbalances caused by an inadequate market mechanism. British nationalisation has, however, been criticised for precisely this reason — it was too economistic. Indeed, it is argued that nationalisation in Britain failed, to the extent that it did, because there was insufficient politics (democracy) injected into its application and its ends.

Tracing the pattern of nationalisation in Third World countries, where less success was achieved, it shows a similar trend to South Africa. In most Latin American and African countries studied, nationalisation was primarily a means for achieving political ends — such as self-determination. While self-determination has a strong economic component, it is primarily an issue of power — who decides on the future of industrial sectors. Judging by the record of nationalisation in these countries, there was not enough emphasis on the economic goals.

Too little economics

Of the 18 economic aims of nationalisation elsewhere in the world, only eight are included in South Africa so far. No new ones have been included. The question is why? Perhaps because economic policy is still in the making. Perhaps only when the proponents of nationalisation are in government will they become practical, rather than rhetorical, about the economic issues. It also reflects the starting point for the debate — nationalisation was stated as a given, rather than fitted into economic policies. Most of the aims in South Africa are macro-economic in nature. Few are micro-economic (for the benefit of the firm itself). In other parts of the world the needs of companies are emphasised — attaining structural efficiencies, responding to a crisis in profitability, savings on economies of scale, meeting competition world-wide, developing the value chain. Again, this reflects a lack of attention, from the advocates of nationalisation, to what it takes to make individual companies profitable, a fact for which these people are continually attacked.

The economic problems manifest themselves most in the black community as poverty, homelessness, low wages and unemployment. The organisations which are responding to their membership at this level are the ANC, SACP and Cosatu. The solution to those problems will be found in developing coherent and workable macro-economic, long-term plans. That, in turn, will depend upon a thorough understanding of the dynamics of different industries and how the economy works at a micro-economic level. Already the ANC and Cosatu are engaged in such research. It is likely, therefore, that this will inform the way these groups respond to the needs not only of their members, but the economy as a whole.

Some of the aims are also the product of immediate self-interest. For example, Cosatu emphasises the need for worker control, industrial democracy, changing employment practices, preserving and creating employment, and the productivity benefits that would result. While not questioning the validity of these demands, they represent the interest of only a section of the population in nationalisation. This is not to suggest that Cosatu bears little regard for those outside the factory gates. However, the articulated aims of nationalisation reflect the interests of workers inside the factory. This is correct, given that Cosatu was set up with the express function of representing those interests. Other sectors of the population — like consumers — are still to find their voice on the issue because they are less organised. When they do, the expectations on nationalisation will change.

Nationalisation has not yet been incorporated into an economic programme and the aims are being discussed in the abstract. To the extent that nationalisation has been considered as part of an economic programme, it has simply been said that it will be considered as one option; or that nationalisation (in the given programme) will be likely or unlikely. Thus the debate as it stands remains at the abstract level, which is fertile ground for heated, emotional debates. If the proponents of nationalisation wish to win more support for their aims, they will have to become more specific about what it can achieve outside of purely political targets. Until then they will be accused of being naive and unrealistic.

The subjectivity of the debate is bad for another reason: 20 years after the nationalisation, the question will be asked 'was nationalisation a success?'. If the aims that were originally set out were not measurable (see Appendix 3.1), it will be impossible to judge. Inevitably, the macro-economic, politicised emphasis is likely to affect the way nationalisation would be implemented, and the forms nationalised industries would take. It will also make it difficult to judge the success of nationalisation 20 years down the line.

Notes

1. African National Congress and Congress of South African Trade Unions, 'Recommendations on Post-Apartheid Economic Policy', ANC-Cosatu, Johannesburg, 1990, p3.

2. Lenin, VI, *On Workers' Control and the Nationalisation of Industry*, Progress Publishers, Moscow, 1982, p12.
3. Harris, L, 'The Mixed Economy of A Democratic South Africa', paper delivered at the Lausanne Colloquium of the Institute For Social Development, University of the Western Cape, as part of the Research Programme of Economic Research on South Africa (Erosa), Switzerland, 1989, p3.
4. Murray, R, 'Ownership, Control and the Market' in *New Left Review*, July/August 1987.
5. Ingram, GM, *Expropriation of US Property in South America: Nationalization of Oil and Copper Companies in Peru, Bolivia and Chile,* Prager, New York, 1974.
6. Curwen, PJ, *Public Enterprise: A Modern Approach,* Harvester, London, 1986, pp31-32.
7. Curwen, *Public Enterprise*, pp31-32.
8. Welsh, F, *The Profit of The State: Nationalised Industries and Public Enterprises,* Maurice Temple Smith, London, 1982, p209.
9. Curwen, *Public Enterprise*, pp32-33.
10. Davies, R, 'Nationalisation, Socialisation and the Freedom Charter', *South African Labour Bulletin*, 12(2), 1987.
11. Slovo, J, Interview by the author, 1990, p9.
12. *Weekly Mail* 23/2/90.
13. Erwin, A, 'An Economic Policy Framework', unpublished draft paper, 1990, p35.
14. African National Congress, 'Constitutional Guidelines For A Democratic South Africa' in *Joining the ANC, An Introductory Handbook to The African National Congress*, ANC Publications, Johannesburg, 1990, pp66-67.
15. ANC-Cosatu, 'Recommendations on Post-Apartheid Economic Policy', 1990.
16. *Sowetan*, 5/3/90.
17. Riordan, R, 'The Nationalisation of Industry in South Africa', in *Monitor*, April 1990, p102.
18. Mandela, N, 'Statement of the Deputy-President of the African National Congress, Nelson Mandela, at the Consultative Business Movement Conference: Options for Building an Economic Future', Johannesburg, 1990, p8.
19. Walter Sisulu, quoted in *Sunday Times*, 11/3/90
20. Nicol, M, 'The Case for Nationalising the Mines', in *Weekly Mail*, 30/3/90.
21. African National Congress, 'Freedom Charter, Adopted At Kliptown, 26th June, 1955 at The Congress Of The People' in *Joining the ANC, An Introductory Handbook to The African National Congress*, ANC Publications, Johannesburg, 1990, p60.
22. Mandela, Statement to Consultative Business Movement Conference: Options for Building an Economic Future, 1990, pp9-10.
23. Erwin, 'An Economic Policy Framework', p35.
24. Nicol, 'The Case for Nationalising the Mines'.
25. ANC, 'Constitutional Guide Lines For A Democratic South Africa', p66.
26. *The Star*, 19/2/90.
27. ANC-Cosatu, 'Recommendations on Post-Apartheid Economic Policy', 1990.
28. *New Nation*, 2/3/90.
29. Mbongwa, M, and Nhlapo-Lewis, K, 'Towards a Mixed Economy in South African Agriculture', paper prepared for the ANC-Cosatu Conference on the Post-Apartheid Economy, Harare, April 1990, pp19-20, (emphasis added).
30. Sangweni, S, 'Impact of Agriculture and Rural Development among the Blacks in South Africa'. Paper for the ANC-Cosatu Conference on the Post-Apartheid Economy, Harare, April 1990, p5.
31. Mbongwa and Nhlapo-Lewis, 'Towards a Mixed Economy in South African Agriculture', p20.

CHAPTER TWO

THE TARGETS

The Freedom Charter is the only existing document which attempts to tackle the question of what should be nationalised. But even that is vague. The fact is, advocates of nationalisation in South Africa have only a hazy idea of their targets — the large companies, the conglomerates, the land, the banks. They would be extremely hard pressed to state precisely which companies they would nationalise and why. It has been enough for the debate to centre on the 'principle' of whether or not to nationalise.

This is inadequate. Loud, unspecified threats of nationalisation cause deep unease and confusion in the business sector. More important, generalised statements of this kind ignore the fact that the feasibility of nationalisation hinges on the need to be accurate, clear and specific. Careful, reasoned and systematic selection of companies or assets is an essential part — perhaps *the* essential part — of any nationalisation strategy. Does a sober selection method exist?

THE POSSIBLE TARGETS OF THE FREEDOM CHARTER

Let us take the Freedom Charter as a starting point. What would be nationalised if its proposals were implemented? It targets banks, mines and monopoly industry. (The word nationalisation is not actually used, but is generally taken by Charterists in the ANC alliance to be the intention). Major South African banks include:

- Commercial banking groups: Standard Bank Investment Corporation; First National Bank; Nedcor; Bankorp; Volkskas.

● Merchant banks: Finansbank; First National Corporate and Investment Bank; Investec; Rand Merchant Bank; Senbank (Central Merchant Bank); Standard Merchant Bank; UAL Merchant Bank; Volkskas Merchant Bank.

The above list does not include other financial intermediaries such as building societies, unit trusts, life assurers, short-term insurers and savings institutions such as pension funds and medical aids and the Freedom Charter does not specifically call for the nationalisation of these companies, although this might have been intended when it was drafted in the 1950s. If this is the inference, Sage, the largest financial services company in South Africa, which is larger and more powerful than many banks, would no doubt be seen as a target in the Charter's terms.

The mining industry can be broken down into the following sectors:

● Gold — the 34 major gold mines, owned by six mining houses, Anglo American, General Mining, Anglo Vaal, Gold Fields, Johannesburg Consolidated Investments (controlled by Anglo), and Rand Mines, together produce more gold than any other country, and are South Africa's largest foreign exchange earner.

● Coal — the four major producers, Anglo American Coal, Witbank Collieries, Trans-Natal, and Gold Fields Coal — are all controlled by the large mining houses.

● Energy Minerals — besides coal this includes hydrocarbon fuels and uranium.

● Precious metals and minerals include diamonds, platinum and silver.

● Metallic mines — South Africa has world dominance in chrome and vanadium. Other minerals produced include aluminium, antimony, beryllium, cobalt, copper, iron, lead, manganese, molybdenum, nickel, silicon, tin, tungsten and zinc.

● Non-metallic minerals include alumino-silicates, asbestos, dimension stone, feldspar, fluorspar, gypsum, limestone and lime, magnesium and magnesite, mica, potash, pyrite, salt, special clays, tiger's eye and vermiculite.

The large mining houses dominate production of precious, energy, metallic and non-metallic minerals. There are, however, a few smaller producers, particularly in the non-metallic sector.

● Mining financials — these companies do not produce minerals, but are investment and holding companies with portfolios in the mining sector. They are usually the vehicles through which the large mining houses control subsidiary mines.

'Monopoly industry' is less easy to define. A monopoly, in the strict sense of the term, produces or sells the entire output of some commodity. The term is usually used more loosely than that. In the United States a firm is considered a monopoly if it accounts for more than 33% of market sales. What the Freedom Charter presumably refers to is the phenomenon of the 'oligopoly', where a small number of firms exercise a particularly high degree of control or ownership in a given market. Those firms would account for a large proportion of turnover, employment, profits, assets and so on. There is also an acknowledgement by those few firms of their dominance, and their mutual impact on the market. Thus, if cartels are not formed, there is at least a calculation as to what effect each move within a market will have on competitors. These large firms have a mutual interest in maintaining a stable, growing market where uncertainty and strong competition is not the order of the day.[1] There are also some classic monopolies in South Africa with entire industries dominated by one player:

- The beer industry, where South African Breweries, owned and controlled by Anglo American, accounts for over 95% of the market consumption, and a larger proportion of its profits;
- The diamond industry — De Beers has a world monopoly on the marketing of diamonds, and controls almost all of diamond production in Southern Africa;
- The tobacco industry, where Rembrandt dominates the local tobacco market;
- The hotel industry, where Southern Suns owns and controls a majority of three, four and five star hotels (excluding those in the bantustans);
- Glass production, where Pilkingtons and Plate Glass have a monopoly on production and marketing respectively;
- Commercial explosives, all manufactured in one factory, the Modderfontein Dynamite factory owned by African Explosives and Chemical Industries (AECI).

There are, in addition, some government-owned monopolies. These include Eskom (electricity), Transnet (railway and air transport), the post office (post and telecommunications), Armscor (weapons and munitions), nuclear energy and nuclear research, and a range of services including water and sewerage.

The majority of South African industry is characterised by oligopoly. In some sectors these include government-owned industry (oil and gas, steel, food marketing). In most sectors, however, there are a few firms in control which are owned either privately or through the Johannesburg Stock Exchange. Such sectors include food production and distribution, retail and wholesale, furniture, gold, coal and other mining, sugar, beverages, banks and financial services, building and construction, printing, packaging and publishing, and pharmaceuticals.

The oligopolies do not stop at the level of different sectors of industry. Through the JSE, control over those oligopolies can be traced to an even smaller number of companies. According to Robin McGregor's *Who Owns Whom*, Anglo American, Sanlam, Old Mutual, Anglo Vaal, Rembrandt and Liberty Life between them control over 80% of South Africa's market capitalisation.

An interpretation of the Freedom Charter says it will be necessary 'at an early stage' to gain control of the parent boards of the large corporations. 'This should provide for a substantial measure of real control over ... the vast bulk of capitalist production without having immediately to take over the management of each of the hundreds of component enterprises.'[2]

Strictly speaking, therefore, few companies would fall into the category of monopoly. There would be more — at a higher level of conglomeration — which would be targeted by the Freedom Charter, but defining monopoly as oligopoly.

Nationalisations in other countries have incorporated a wide range of companies and activities, usually in essential goods or services. Most often nationalisation has involved companies providing infrastructure for both producers and consumers and which provide the necessities of life. (See Table 2)

TABLE 2: Examples of overseas nationalisations in different sectors

Company	Sector	Country	Reasons
Anglo-Iranian Oil	Oil	UK	Strategic, military
British National Oil	Oil	UK	Maximise revenue
Statoil	Oil	Norway	Maximise revenue,strategic
Compagnie Francaise des Petroles	Oil	France	Strategic
Ente Nazionale Idrocarburi (ENI)	Oil, gas	Italy	Strategic, bankruptcy
British Gas	Gas	UK	Bankruptcy, rationalise
Ente Partecipazioni e Finanziamento Industria Manifatturiera (EFIM)	Agriculture, engineering	Italy	Macro-economic, stabilise
Pescaperu	Fishing	Peru	Foreign exchange, defensive
United Fruit	Agriculture, cattle, cans	Cuba	Ideological, defensive
Instituto per la Ricostruzione Industriale (IRI)	Multi-sector	Italy	Rationalise, modernise, strategic, bankruptcy
Tennessee Valley Authority	Electricity	USA	Strategic, public interest
Reconstruction Finance	Finance	USA	Strategic, war
Banque de France	Finance	France	Investment capacity
National Coal Board	Coal	UK	No profit, rationalise consumer benefit
Amtrak	Railways	USA	Bankruptcy
Conrail	Railways	USA	Bankruptcy
British Rail	Railways	UK	Efficiency, economy of scale, public need
SNCF	Railways	France	Consumer benefit, strategic
British Air	Air transport	UK	Prestige, strategic
River Transport	Transport	Burma	Self-determination
Universal Suez Maritime Canal Co	Shipping	Egypt	Self-determination
British Broadcasting	TV, radio	UK	Diversity of service, public accountability
Rolls Royce, British Leyland	Motor	UK	Bankruptcy
Central Electricity Board	Electricity	UK	Abuse of monopoly power
Kenecott/Anaconda	Copper	Chile	Self-determination, monopoly power
Compania Agricola	Agriculture	Guatemala	Self-determination, monopoly power
Cerro Corporation	Mines, transport	Peru	Self-determination, monopoly power

Table 2 shows many sectors as possible targets of nationalisation. However, targets need not be selected at random. Economists who have considered the prospect of nationalisation have become more systematic in their approach to targeting companies or sectors.

The 1945 programme of the British Labour Party introduced a new term into the nationalisation vocabulary — 'commanding heights'. It developed criteria to assess which companies fell within the ambit for possible nationalisation. Initially, this approach identified key companies in the most important sectors of the economy. Usually, the commanding heights were occupied by one or two very large companies which could, by virtue of their strategic position, influence the entire economy and its growth and distribution patterns.

Since then the debate about which companies should be nationalised has become more sophisticated. The commanding heights concept has remained a key guide, the argument being that the target of a nationalisation programme should be the commanding heights of a sector, not just a random selection of important, big or monopoly companies.

IDENTIFYING THE COMMANDING HEIGHTS

Murray[3] asserts that the key feature of a commanding height is the point where it achieves control over the whole sector. This is something which the Mengistu government did not take into account when nationalising the largest 150 companies in Ethiopia.It thought that achieving its aims of redistribution and self-determination rested simply upon nationalising the biggest companies — that this was the route to the commanding heights. However, nationalisation did not change the companies' technological dependence on their foreign parent corporations, it just allowed a re-negotiation of the terms of that dependence. Profits were still drawn out of those Ethiopian firms by variations in the price of inputs or in sliding-scale payments on the management contracts.

This reflected a development within large manufacturing corporations which shifted control away from direct ownership to control by contract. Coca-Cola, for example, does not own bottling plants, but controls the soft-drink market through patents and contracts. In this context some multinational commodity producers have actually welcomed nationalisation of their primary assets, or sold them off to local concerns.

> These multinationals have instead consolidated around the supply of primary product technology, of advanced management systems, and of international marketing, and/or have developed synthetic substitutes which can be produced in first world factories rather than Third World land.[4]

Zambia provides another well-known example of a country which unsuccessfully tried to gain control over its key economic sector — the copper mines. It tried to nationalise the mines, the country's largest employer of labour and earner of foreign exchange. But nationalising the mines did not give the Zambian government control over a key part of the economic chain — the overseas markets. It was also unable to break the dependence on Anglo American because it simply did not have the equipment, the capital and the expertise to run the mines.

Thus, well before nationalising, a government must carefully study the production process, the sector, the international links and the entire value chain. Otherwise, in nationalising what appears to be the biggest company or the largest earner, a government may gain control

> over a lowland plain rather than a commanding height... If control can be monopolized over a key segment of the circuit, then it can be exercised over the rest of the circuit, whether or not it is matched by ownership.[5]

Where there is globally dispersed production, nationalisation only gives control over one point in the chain. Where production, marketing, research and development are not integrated the possibility for expanding social control through nationalisation is correspondingly diminished.

The implication of this approach for South Africa is that companies should not be targeted for nationalisation on sheer size alone, as the Freedom Charter tends to do. Rather, in-depth analysis of each sector needs to be undertaken before the commanding height can be identified. Five categories have been isolated to identify commanding heights.

The nature of goods or services produced

Where almost every sector of the economy depends on certain products, these become targets for nationalisation on the basis that public ownership is the 'best way to ensure that the crucial material inputs for all other industries are available to support the overall pattern of development the state wishes to see.'[6] In South Africa, provision of key materials for many different sectors was one of the main reasons the National Party government and its predecessors chose to develop nationalised industries such as Eskom and Iscor.

Sugar and chemicals are two random examples of sectors which fit this definition. The sugar industry is dominated by Tongaat-Hulett, a subsidiary of Anglo American. Besides being one of the top 20 industrial companies, Tongaat produces a commodity crucial to over 250 other production processes. Thus a single company is in total command of the sugar industry. There are few indigenous companies in the crucial chemical sector dominated by foreign-owned (mainly US) companies. Chemicals produced are used in everything from food to motor tyres to paint and pharmaceuticals.

Command of finance for investment

A nationalisation programme could contain centralised state corporations which include banks, other credit institutions and those sectors which operate in large, closely interrelated units or have a monopoly position. In South Africa these centralising bodies would be the financial and mining sectors and some large businesses which potentially control investment.

This is relevant when considering whether the banks, mining finance houses and other monopolies should be nationalised on economic grounds. While there is no guarantee that the state will invest wisely, the task of the post-apartheid state will be to ensure that economic surplus is invested to build a system that is not based on racial discrimination, which will foster competitive advantage, and redirect the economy away from its dependence on minerals.

Mining finance houses have been the major source of investment capital in South Africa. Commercial banks have primarily been conduits for mining profits and channels for directing investment into either productive or speculative activity. 'Nationalisation of these institutions would give the state direct control of this surplus and ensure it is invested wisely to restructure the economy.'[7]

As evidence, Harris points to Anglo's huge expansion of the Free State gold fields which affected the entire South African economic development pattern after World War Two. When the development was complete, at the start of the 1960s, Anglo decided to invest in the modernisation and expansion of the manufacturing sector, increasing its manufacturing interests fivefold in eight years. Part of the case for nationalising Anglo American is that it has the power, through its control of vast amounts of investment capital, to shape and direct South Africa's economic path. A similar case can be made for nationalising banks and other economic giants.

Gelb argues that South Africa's future growth path should be based on state mobilisation of the nation's investment. The government should achieve a 'redistribution of investment'[8] since investment will be the generator of growth. To achieve this, the conglomerates cannot be left in their present form.

There could be a simpler solution, with a significant portion of South Africa's economy controlled by a democratic state taking over two mutual life associations, Old Mutual and Sanlam. These associations, 'by virtue of their greatly diversified investment portfolios, have a more relevant sway over the economy than the Anglo American-De Beers alliance.'[9]

It remains an open question whether control over investment capital would be best achieved by nationalisation. Neither Barrett nor Gelb advocate nationalisation. Erwin goes so far as to say that nationalising these institutions 'would be an act of bureaucratic suicide for a future government.'[10]

Employing labour

Equally suicidal is the simplistic notion that eradicating apartheid at its root will involve nationalising the companies which control employment practices. Hiring, firing, organisation of production, and training are based upon racial divisions and are, of course, at the heart of apartheid. It may be useful to note who is employing whom, but not as a criterion for selecting targets for nationalisation! Excluding agriculture, the large employers of labour in South Africa are the following:

- General government, which employs 25% of non-agricultural workers;
- Manufacturing, which employs 26% of non-agricultural workers;
- The mines, which employ 16% of non-agricultural workers;
- Trade employs 14%;
- Public transport, post and communications employ 6%;
- Construction employs 6%.

Within mining there are 740 000 employees of which nearly 500 000 work in gold mines and over 100 000 in coal mines. Most employees work for one of the six mining houses identified above. The large employers in manufacturing are listed in Table 3.[11]

TABLE 3: Major employers in the manufacturing sector according to industrial group

Company	Employees	Sector	Controller
Barlows	159 800	Ind Holding	SA Mutual
CG Smith	95 000	Food	SA Mutual
SA Breweries	85 000	Bev & Hotels	Anglo American
Malbak	63 000	Ind Holding	Sanlam
CGS Food	61 000	Food	SA Mutual
Iscor	58 000	Steel	Government
Murray and Roberts	47 000	Construction	Sanlam
Tradegro	46 000	Retail, wholesale	Sanlam
Anglo American Industrial Corp	44 000	Ind Holding	Anglo American
Anglo Vaal Indus	41 000	Ind Holding	Anglo Vaal
Tongaat-Hullett	40 000	Sugar	Anglo American
Safren	38 500	Ind Holding	Sanlam
Premier Group	33 000	Food	Anglo American
Tiger Oats	32 000	Food	SA Mutual
Federale Volksbeleggings	31 000	Ind Holding	Sanlam

There are another eight companies employing over 20 000 each, including Sasol, Metkor, AECI, Pick 'n Pay, OK Bazaars, Dorbyl, Nampak and Sappi.

Foreign exchange earners

South Africa, as a Third World economy, has become economically dependent on raw material production. Minerals have become the backbone of the economy, contributing nearly 13% to the Gross Domestic Product in 1988, and accounting for 55% of total exports. Metals contributed another 30% of exports.[12]

Using the commanding heights concept, it seems reasonable to consider the centrality of certain sectors to the efficient and profitable functioning of the economy. Certainly, this has been the case with many nationalisations (copper and tin in Chile, and copper in Zambia).

International companies

Unlike other Third World nationalisations, foreign companies are unlikely to be nationalised in South Africa. No serious advocates have proposed nationalising multinational or foreign companies.

The sanctions campaign against the South African government meant foreign corporations in South Africa kept a low profile. As such their dominant role within the economy was not visible to the extent that is true, say, of Anglo American. But they do dominate certain key sectors, such as electronics, chemicals and oil, and this is likely to become apparent to any future government. It is possible that those considering nationalisation have been deterred from turning their attention to foreign companies out of fear of severe retribution from the international community. But if nationalisation is to be prompted by the commanding heights logic, then the issue must be confronted sooner or later.

LAND

> We have demanded that the land be returned to those who work it... We are concerned with the principle of an equitable distribution of the land, and what will be done with specific farmers is a question to be determined...[13]

Mandela's formulation, in line with the Freedom Charter, implies that all farmers could be a target for nationalisation. At its broadest it has been argued that all agricultural land could become subject to a land claim, given that the present (white) owners seized the land through colonial conquest. Even owner-occupier farmers actively involved on the farm could be subject to a land claim.[14]

Most targets for land nationalisation from Charterist ranks are more specific and include:

- Agribusiness, and farms owned by 'monopolies' (ie Anglo American and others);
- Land presently occupied by farmers who gained control over that land by virtue of forced removals or legislative decree by the National Party government. In other words, the individuals are less the target than the land itself;
- Land belonging to absentee landlords, but which is farmed using a system of labour tenancy;
- Under-utilised land;
- State land — while not often mentioned, the state itself has vast tracts of land currently being used for purposes as diverse as forestry, land speculation, military testing grounds and security.

Companies owned 16% of agricultural land in 1983. About 13% of agricultural land was owned by private companies, most of which in turn are individuals or small groups, rather than unquoted subsidiaries of large companies. The average farm owned by publicly owned companies is large — on average 5 511 hectares compared to 1 435 hectares in 1983 for other commercial farms.[15]

If monopolies are the target, these smaller private companies would presumably not be at risk. However, some advocate that all land owned by public companies should be nationalised: 'Farms owned by public companies and absentee landlords should, in principle, be nationalised. This includes the land, the farm buildings and the means of production.'[16]

The state could expropriate limited categories of land and reserve it for occupation by, and possible resale to, resource-poor individual farmers or farming communities. Such categories could include land occupied over a long period by labour tenants, black-spot land expropriated in terms of the National Party government's programmes, or 'abandoned' land.

One of the targets for land nationalisation would be 'under-utilised' land. The question is how to identify under-utilisation? Current versus potential utilisation cannot be a measure because production levels are not static. Furthermore,

> the announcement of a policy of expropriating under-utilised land could either cause existing owners to increase output, if the terms of compensation were thought to be unfavourable, or to reduce output if the opposite were thought to be the case.[17]

MEETING THE AIMS

In the light of the aims of nationalisation outlined in the previous chapter, there are other considerations in drawing up a list of potential targets for nationalisation.

THE TARGETS

Correcting racial imbalances and achieving industrial democracy does not imply industry-specific targets. All industries, large or small, are potential targets. But this does not mean all industries would be nationalised.

Attempts to shift decision making to a group responsible to the public probably applies particularly to commodities and services most used and needed by the public, and without which their quality of life would be materially threatened. These include electricity, hospitals, sewerage — many of which are already government controlled.

Besides the land question, the aim of national self-determination means possible nationalisation of some key economic sectors controlled by multinationals. These could be some chemical, electronic and other high-tech companies.

Targets for re-nationalisation include enterprises recently privatised by the present government, such as Iscor, several marketing boards, several game and city parks, and some hospitals.

If redistribution is the aim, it might be tempting to nationalise companies which continually generate large profits. A nationalising government could identify the 'cash cows' in each sector and simply milk their large cash flows. But nationalising cash cows could be short-sighted if the subsequent implications for other businesses in the conglomerate portfolios are not taken into account; if reinvestment needs are not met; or if it will jeopardise future investment in new ventures. Natural monopolies which could be nationalised include railways, roads, health services, electricity, gas and others.

Given that South Africa is in the midst of an economic crisis (reflected in the slow rate of growth, high rates of inflation and unemployment, and the increasing numbers of insolvencies) it may happen that the government is invited to nationalise a company. The present government has been asked to step in to assist troubled companies where the private sector is unable (or unwilling) to do so. The most notable recent cases were Nedbank and the ERPM mine. In both cases the government did step in, but without itself taking a stake in those companies. An alternative strategy might be for the government to nationalise large, important companies experiencing a crisis of profitability.

Obviously not all companies with profitability problems would be targets. For example, there are 18 marginal gold mines, and there would be great temptation for the mining houses to hand over troubled mines to the government instead of trying to restore profitability. Furthermore, several hundred companies are declared insolvent every year. There would have to be some yardstick by which to judge which companies should be bailed out, and which left to the vagaries of the market mechanism.

Taking over failed companies is the one form of nationalisation which might be acceptable to business people — indeed one notable example of why it is quite wrong to view nationalisation in strictly emotive, ideological terms!

TARGETING COMPANIES FOR NATIONALISATION

It should already be clear that nationalisation is a high-risk strategy. If targets are key economic sectors and the commanding heights within each sector, then the proposal means the state takes over the foundation of the economy as well as determining its future. If the commanding heights are to be nationalised, then the state had better make sure it can keep the sector working — failing which the whole sector, and indeed a large part of the entire economy, may be destroyed.

From the question 'which companies?' emerges another key question: 'how do you identify which companies?' The method used to target companies for nationalisation becomes fundamental. The Freedom Charter is more a statement of intent and an outline of aspirations, than an economic programme. It does not propose detailed methods of achieving its aims but it does propose targets.

In the 1950s certain clauses of the Freedom Charter attempted to single out the key sectors of the South African economy which, if nationalised, would assist in achieving its broader political and economic aims. Perhaps these selections were symbolic — the wealth (mines), the money (banks), the power (monopolies) and the heritage (land).

While the Freedom Charter does not claim to present a rigorous economic blueprint, it can be a guide in two important areas: it points to the central importance of being able to mobilise investment capital, and highlights the key place monopolies have in the economy.

As pointed out earlier, this definition of monopolies includes true monopolies (such as South African Breweries or De Beers), oligopolies (of which Anglo is the largest) and natural monopolies which are, for the most part, already nationalised.

If one starts with the aims of nationalisation spelled out by Freedom Charter proponents, and then deduce which companies will be needed to achieve those aims:

- The targets will be politically determined — the choices based more on political considerations, than on sound economics, primarily because the aims of nationalisation are highly politicised;
- Even if the imbalance in the aims was corrected, there would be a tendency towards the 'shotgun' approach, where every company that might achieve those diverse aims would be targeted.

This approach is therefore inadequate.

Land nationalisation

The moral arguments for nationalising land are undoubtedly compelling. The 1913 Land Act removed land from those 'to whom it historically belonged.' The heritage of decades of homeland policies is mass starvation, land degradation and other products of overpopulation. Because of the pressures this has caused, pro-nationalisation groups aim for instant relief of that suffering and misery. Economic growth and philosophies are secondary considerations.

If one uses these arguments as a starting point, the targeting is easy. Certain areas of land — such as black spots — would be selected on the basis that they were illegitimately seized in the name of apartheid. Similarly, with tenant farmers and absentee landlords, it would not be difficult to justify the nationalisation. Land that has long been owned for the sole purpose of speculation could also fall into the ambit of this argument.

However, after those initial moral positions have been exhausted, the process of targeting land to nationalise becomes less easy. What happens to under-utilised land, agribusiness and large private landholdings? The moral arguments do not provide a satisfactory answer. The commanding heights approach is also not suitable for this sector, particularly if it is to be characterised by subsistence or small-scale co-operative farming.

Modifying the commanding heights method

The 'old socialist' approach made it easy to target companies for nationalisation: quite simply, *all* companies should be nationalised. However, with the failure of that approach, the 'new socialism' tried to work out a more coherent and selective approach. 'Commanding heights' was the result.

This method, based on a macro-economic logic, has become the most systematic method for identifying the targets of nationalisation. However, it is still in the process of development, and can be used only as a starting point, to focus on those companies which, if nationalised, would most likely produce the desired aims (unlocking wealth, investment potential, redistributing power and so on).

What the commanding heights approach does reveal is the difference between nationalising what is *strategic* and what is *big*. At this stage of the debate in South Africa the targets of nationalisation are the big corporations. While these corporations may in the end be targeted, commanding heights logic suggests that this should not be a starting point. In other words, in South Africa the approach should not be: 'let us take over that company/conglomerate. Then we will work out why, and what we can do with it.'

This happened in many Third World countries where companies were nationalised because they were big and foreign. While this might have been a legitimate political reason for countries engaged in a struggle for self-determination, it usually led to economic dead-ends.

There also remains a divergence between the approach which recommends taking over the key sectors and that which advocates nationalisation of companies for more pragmatic reasons — companies better run under public control; companies which are socially required but which cannot be run profitably; companies which have collapsed, but are so important economically that they require rescue; and companies required for strategic reasons.

The commanding heights approach fails to consider these pragmatic issues. This flies in the face of its original motivation — to find an underlying logic which would guide government in a unified, coherent programme of selection. Looking to economic areas in which the future government would like to become the motor of growth seems to fit better with the goals of economic growth. Gold and other minerals and metals have been the backbone of the past. However, there is agreement amongst most economists that those sectors are unlikely to provide new growth in future.

The commanding heights concept should be forward looking — otherwise a nationalising government may well end up entrenching dead weight as the centre of the economy, and the most backward parts of our economy as the centre of the state's enterprise. Thus, the commanding heights concept can be reinterpreted to refer to those parts of the economy which will be the engines of *future growth*. What these will be is difficult to predict.[18]

The state may find itself in a position where it has nationalised a whole series of cash-hungry companies in highly competitive, growing markets. These may well be the 'future growth points' of a new economy, or the commanding heights of a sector. In such a case the state will have to pump in money from tax income or other public funds.

Thus, further selection criteria are necessary, which consider the economic viability of the acquisitions, and their workability as a 'portfolio'.

Focusing on the commanding heights is far more systematic and will end in a narrower range of better-chosen targets. But the method is not sufficiently developed, and nowhere has it been adequately developed or theorised as a comprehensive planning tool in itself.

The inadequacies in the commanding heights method can perhaps be overcome. Set out below are elements of a methodology which could be developed in targeting commanding heights companies for nationalisation.

Asking the right questions

Using the commanding heights idea as a starting point, it is possible to examine which companies are strategic to nationalise from several points of view:

- What are the growth areas of the future economy? Taking over a declining industry or one which offers no growth potential is useless;
- How key is the sector to the economy, and which is the key company in its sector? (Criteria for deciding what is 'key' would need to be set out);
- What are the key areas of economic activity which are going to generate that growth? Which are the key companies within that area?
- How competitive is the company in the world market, or how competitive could it become? Who are the key competitors, and what will it take to match or better their efforts?
- Why are those companies key — for sheer size, or because of good management of the critical success factors, for expertise, or other factors?
- Does the company occupy the dominant point in the value chain, or is it dependent on other processes, be they inputs or outputs, which it does not control? For example, chemicals are used in many production processes in South Africa, but practically the entire chemical sector operates on patent agreements with US and other firms. Nationalising those companies, however key they appear, would gain control over some machinery, a few skilled people, but not chemicals;
- What are the long-term projections for different industries? Taking over the gold mines is all very well. But there are only another 30 or 40 years of gold left in the ground, and at least 20 of those will use the surplus to pay off the original purchase;
- Is the product key to other important sectors? How does it affect the cost of other products and the functioning of other sectors? While a product like steel is not a high growth sector, it is vitally important in almost every production process;
- Does the company command a high proportion of finance available for investment? As has been mentioned gold production is a non-growth area, and has limited long-term potential. Yet mining finance houses command huge capital resources which can be employed strategically elsewhere in the economy;
- Does the company employ a significant number of workers? By itself this factor is not important enough to warrant the company being targeted for nationalisation. However, it is a contributing factor;
- Does the company generate large earnings of foreign exchange? Anglo American Gold, while not in a long-term growth sector, produces 40% of the country's gold, and thus a substantial portion of its foreign earnings;
- What could be achieved by nationalising the company that could not be achieved with private ownership?

When planning how to construct a strong state sector, pro-nationalisation groupings in South Africa always look at the companies or sectors to be controlled by the state. But which sectors or industries should the state *not* have? This issue must form an implicit part of the planning process to construct a powerful and efficient state sector. A combination of nationalisation and privatisation, in which the economic and not the political selection criteria are uppermost, is one option an imaginative government might consider.

Study the company

As with any merger or acquisition process, a company should be investigated to see what its strengths and weaknesses really are — and not just those on paper. More importantly, the reasons behind its present strength or weakness should be revealed. It is therefore advisable to study the company in minute detail before putting it on any nationalisation list. Some suggestions for what this examination should include are:

- A full financial analysis, including an historic analysis (using ratios of liquidity, asset management, debt management, profitability), investment decision analysis, an analysis of financing decisions, dividend payments (if applicable), working capital management, share price and trading analysis (if applicable), and the risk profile of the company;
- An analysis of turnover, contribution, operating profit by product type, exports and geographical market;
- An analysis of the technology and production base, looking at the process technology used, production methods involved, purchasing, inventory systems and so on;
- An analysis of all fixed assets, including their age, rate of depreciation, market value, and suitability for their purpose;
- An analysis of how the company markets its products or services, and to whom. Standard market analysis should include studying the prices, placing, product and promotion;
- Very important in the context of nationalisation is an analysis of company human resources, in both functional and structural aspects, including studying management culture and the industrial relations history of the company. The skills base that exists, and the skills base that is needed in the future should be specified;
- A study of the management information system;
- Again, in the nationalisation context, patents, trademarks, royalty and licensing agreements — both granted to others and granted to the company by others — should be clarified;

● A comparison of all the above with the position and performance of competitors, particularly global competitors;
● Lastly, this study should include a pre-emptive analysis of all defensive tactics that could be employed by owners and management in preventing the nationalisation.

The strategic target decision

A strategic approach to targeting companies could be built upon the factors outlined above. The following contains some of the elements, in summarised form, of such an approach.
● Look at the key sectors of the economy and study in detail their:
 * centrality to the economy
 * growth potential and long-term sustainability
 * impact on other industries
  - cost
  - functioning
  - use of product
 * command over investment capital
 * involvement in employment of labour and job creation
 * earnings of foreign exchange
● Analyse the sector itself:
 * competitiveness in the world market
 * find the dominant point in the value chain
 * do an industry and competitor analysis
● Analyse the targeted company in detail.
● Test the wisdom of nationalisation with known management techniques. For example, use portfolio analysis to achieve the best possible combination of state companies.

Using the suggested method for targeting companies for nationalisation will result in a far more specific, limited list of companies. As a result of the process of selection, and in the course of the investigations into the company, there will be increased clarity as to the purpose and possibilities of nationalising a particular company. This will impact upon the performance targets which are later set down, as well as help formulate workable yardsticks by which to judge the success or failure of the state enterprise in the medium and longer term.

NOTES

1. Bannock, G, Baxter, RE, and Rees, R, *A Dictionary of Economics*, Penguin Books, Middlesex, 1972, p303.
2. Davies, R, 'Nationalisation, Socialisation and the Freedom Charter' in *South African Labour Bulletin* 12(2), 1987, p101.
3. Murray, R, 'Ownership, Control and the Market' in *New Left Review*, July/August 1987.
4. Murray, 'Ownership, Control and the Market', p90.
5. Murray, 'Ownership, Control and the Market', p90.
6. Harris, L, 'The Mixed Economy of a Democratic South Africa', paper delivered at the Lausanne Colloquium of the Institute For Social Development, University of the Western Cape, as part of the Research Programme of Economic research on South Africa (Erosa), Switzerland, 1989, p5.
7. Harris, 'The Mixed Economy of a Democratic South Africa', p6.
8. Gelb, S, 'Economic Crisis and Growth Models for the Future', paper prepared for the ANC-Cosatu Conference on the Post-Apartheid Economy, Harare, April 1990.
9. Barrett, J, 'The Mutual Path To Welfare', in *The Weekly Mail Supplement*, WM Publications, Johannesburg, 30/3/90, p2.
10. Erwin, A, 'An Economic Policy Framework', unpublished draft paper, 1990, p17.
11. According to the *Financial Mail*, 'Survey of Top Companies', 1990, p123.
12. Republic of South Africa, Department of Mineral and Energy Affairs, Minerals Bureau, 1989, *South Africa's Mineral Industry*, Minerals Bureau, Johannesburg, 1988, p3.
13. Nelson Mandela, quoted in *Business Day*, 21/2/90.
14. Dolny, H, 'Agriculture: Conflicts of Interest in a Mixed Economy', paper prepared for the ANC-Cosatu Conference on the Post-Apartheid Economy, Harare, April 1990.
15. Central Statistical Services, Republic of South Africa, 1983, Census Of Agriculture, Government Printer, Report 06-01021, Pretoria, 1983, p2.
16. Dolny, 'Agriculture: Conflicts of Interest in a Mixed Economy', p17.
17. De Klerk, M, 'Restructuring the Rural Economy: Agricultural Economic Aspects', unpublished working paper for the 'Rural Land' Workshop of The Institute For Democratic Alternatives in South Africa (IDASA), 1989, p29.
18. Porter, ME, *Competitive Advantage: Creating and Sustaining Superior Performance*, Free Press, New York, 1985.

CHAPTER THREE

NATIONALISATION AROUND THE WORLD

The swing to conservative economic policies in European countries and the United States has not, contrary to a prevailing view, discredited the whole concept of nationalisation. In international law and in world forums such as the United Nations, nationalisation is accepted as a legitimate economic tool.

Many countries, often with economies not dissimilar to South Africa's in terms both of GNP and wealth distribution, have tried nationalisation. Success or failure has depended crucially on the manner in which the technical process of nationalisation has been undertaken. Among the key areas have been:

- The process of the acquisition itself;
- How the value of the company has been established;
- Whether or not compensation is paid;
- If there was compensation, the form it has taken and the amount — whether it was considered 'fair' and 'prompt';
- The source of finance.

THE MEXICAN EXPERIENCE, 1934-1947[1]

In 1934 the Cardenas government took its first steps towards nationalising American oil companies. Petromex (now known as Pemex), a government-owned petroleum company was set up and the Nationalisation Law passed. It provided for nationalisation of industries and land where natural resources were threatened, and for the preservation of an enterprise for the public good.

The Cardenas government also aimed to unionise all workers in the oil industry. In 1937 there was a serious clash between oil unions and employers, possibly engineered by the government. When companies refused union demands for wage increases, the government intervened, appointing a negotiating committee. Talks deadlocked, the government declared an 'economic conflict' and launched a full investigation into the oil companies — primarily to see if they could afford to pay the wage increase demanded. The investigation found that the oil companies were making 2,5 times their declared profits because of transfer pricing and creative bookkeeping. The courts ordered massive settlements in the face of petroleum companies protests.

In 1938, at the peak of the crisis, the Mexican government decided to nationalise. Cardenas, the most popular president of the still-ruling — and appropriately named — Institutional Revolutionary Party, struck a powerful populist chord in a message broadcast to the nation when he pronounced that American and British oil companies were to be expropriated for their 'arrogant and rebellious attitude'. Conditions, besides, were ripe for the decision — world war was threatening, and the US likely to become involved; all the necessary legal steps had been taken; ideologically, the government had support; and the oil companies had undermined their own position with profit-skimming practices. Mexicans supported the move enthusiastically, and people from all classes donated money and even jewels to cover the costs of nationalisation.

Valuation, payment and source of finance

The Nationalisation Law specified that compensation was to be based on declared tax value and paid over ten years.

The government repeatedly offered to negotiate the terms of compensation with oil companies. They offered a down payment, with subsequent payments coming out of petroleum export revenues to the amount of the declared tax value of the company installations, plus additional expenditures incurred for investment. Oil companies demanded the return of properties or immediate full payment, plus the value of oil in the ground. The US State Department, keen on an amicable settlement, suggested a marketing agreement.

But the deadlock remained until the oil companies broke ranks. One — Sinclair — accepted compensation of $13-million, $8-million in cash over three years and the remainder in petroleum purchases at a discount over four years.

After the Sinclair settlement, a joint American-Mexican board of experts was set up to settle the compensation issue. The 1938 book value (the value of the assets) of the oil companies was $69-million, although the market value (the value the market places on the firm) was more like $260-million. However, the joint board of experts set the final compensation at just under $24-million plus about $5-million in interest (excluding Sinclair). With additional interest the payments amounted to $30-million to be paid out over five years. A similar agreement was made with the British in 1947.

Mexican 'payment' was not only financial, however. In the course of the negotiations the US scored well out of a series of political trade-offs.

When the Mexican government declared its intention to nationalise, US oil companies took massive counter-action. They boycotted Mexico's oil, denied access to tankers, spare parts, new technology and so on. Production declined. However, domestic consumption of oil increased, new markets were found and the Mexican government managed to win sympathy from American groups. The nationalisation was successful, both economically and politically, and to this day Pemex remains state owned.

THE CUBAN EXPERIENCE, 1957-1963

It has been argued that Cuba's process of nationalisation, socialist policies and alignment to the Soviet Union in the late 1950s was as much the product of US government response to the Cuban Revolution as an ideological commitment to socialism by Castro and the Cuban Communist Party.

Whatever the case, when Castro came to power he initiated a series of economic reforms aimed primarily at redistributing wealth and achieving self-determination. Primary targets were the large US multinational corporations.

In 1959 Castro cancelled a proposed telephone rate increase and appointed an 'interventor' to investigate the telephone company's economic affairs. The US-owned company was ordered to reduce its rural rates by 50%. A 60% royalty was imposed on foreign oil companies, their records were seized, and the government forced oil companies either to drill on their concessions or lose them. (Also in 1959, the Agrarian Reform Law set an upper limit of 995 acres on landholding by any one person, but exceptions up to 3 300 acres were allowed for particularly productive sugar, rice and cattle ranches.)

A law was promulgated allowing the government to take over any companies in financial difficulties or which had reduced production. The US government hit back hard, cutting Cuba's sugar export quota. This was a severe blow to Cuba's foreign exchange earnings. But Cuba announced in 1960 that it would sell sugar to the Soviet Union at favourable terms and open up trade relations generally. This move brought in badly needed capital, machinery and petroleum.

Castro asked Esso, Texaco and Shell to refine the Soviet oil. The oil companies claimed there were technical difficulties, and after consultation with the US government, refused to do so. The Cuban government 'intervened', and proceeded to refine the oil without any problems. The US responded by cutting trade and military agreements, and the rest of the sugar allotment for 1960. According to Sigmund, this was 'more than simply a reprisal for the refinery seizures.' It was an act of economic warfare aimed at 'a change of government' in Cuba.[2]

In March 1960, two American hotels, some agrarian and cattle raising properties owned by United Fruit, and the Moa Bay nickel refinery were intervened after they announced they were ceasing production.

At this stage no companies had been nationalised, neither was wholesale nationalisation planned. The extent of intervention was limited to placing price ceilings, maintaining production where it was being abandoned and limiting the amount of property any one company or individual could own. Despite this, in March 1960, the US government's National Security Council decided to overthrow Castro.

After the second sugar cut, Law 851 was adopted which provided for nationalisation — 'if convenient to the national interest' — of all American-owned property in Cuba. The first nationalisations in Cuba took place in late 1960.

In April 1961 the Bay of Pigs invasion was launched with the aim of overthrowing Castro. When that failed the US closed off all Cuban imports and food shipments to the island were cancelled. By the end of 1961, 75% of Cuban industry and 30% of agriculture were state owned.

In February 1962 a total American embargo on trade was declared. In 1963 remaining Cuban assets in the US were frozen and all dollar transactions with Cuba prohibited.

Valuation, payment and source of finance

The compensation proposed in the Agrarian Reform Law was based on the 1958 declared value for municipal tax purposes and was to be paid in 20-year bonds at

4,5% interest. The US government objected, demanding immediate cash payment, and eventually no compensation was paid for nationalised land.

After the US cut the sugar quota, and under Law 851, compensation for all nationalised property was linked to the re-establishment of trade relations with the US. Cuba offered payment in 30-year bonds at 2% interest. This was to be paid from a special account created by depositing 25% of all dollar income accruing from sugar sales to the US in excess of three million tons at a price of no less than 5,75 cents per pound. It was clear there would be no compensation after the quota cut. The bonds were never printed, and all US properties — about 400 companies — were expropriated. Two Canadian banks were paid for in cash. All existing mortgages on urban real estate were cancelled.

Nationalisation under Law 851 and the establishment of trade relations with the Soviet Union were the last straws for an American government steeped in Cold War ideology. It is unlikely that the Cuban economy would have survived the economic blockade, or that the nationalised industries would have been able to continue running, without vast help from the Soviet Union. The lesson: if conflictual nationalisation happens for a government with a weak economy, it needs a powerful friend to make it work.

THE CHILEAN EXPERIENCE, 1969-1973

Nationalisations in Chile occurred under two successive governments with very different ideologies and methods. Under Frei, a liberal capitalist, a 'Chileanisation' programme was launched for the copper mines. The US government supported the programme and negotiated directly with the companies involved. In 1969 Anaconda, an American mining company, agreed that Chile would acquire majority ownership of the copper mines on the basis of 51% of book value to be paid out over the next 12 years from projected mine profits. Once 60% of the 51% was paid the state then had the option of purchasing the other 49% at a price based on recent earnings. Anaconda would maintain management control until that point, and receive a three-year marketing contract fee of 1% of sales.

Opposition parties in the Frei government objected that this arrangement gave Anaconda the incentive to extract only the most easily available, high quality ore and not undertake conservation measures after 1972. Under the agreement, the Chilean share of profits grew from $200-million in 1968 to $353-million in 1969.

Allende nationalises

Popular Unity (PU), the party of Salvador Allende, went into elections in 1971 on a programme committed to nationalisation of copper, iron, nitrate, coal, banking, steel, cement, petroleum, foreign trade, electricity, transportation, communications, cellulose and paper. This represented a total of 150 enterprises (later reduced to 91) out of 30 000 country-wide. Most parties supported copper nationalisations.

US multinationals such as ITT and Anaconda, as well as the Central Intelligence Agency, the State Department and others teamed up against Allende to stop his election — without success. Immediately upon assuming office Popular Unity began implementing its nationalisation programme, using five methods:

- Copper was first. The nationalisation took place with compensation, under a formula decided by the comptroller-general, less 'excess profits' decided by the president. The companies could appeal the comptroller's decision to a tribunal made up of supreme court judges, the president of the reserve bank and the director of internal revenue. They could not appeal excess profits;
- The second nationalisation method was to authorise the government-owned corporation Corfo to buy out existing owners. Since there was fear of nationalisation, sales were easy to come by on a deferred compensation basis. Iron mines, banks, and nitrate with American links were bought. In the case of domestic banks, Allende gave a two-month period during which shareholders could sell their shares to Corfo at the average price they had commanded in the Chilean stock market at the beginning of 1970 (before the negative effects of the election had made an impact). Most of the banking institutions were acquired in this way;
- Nationalisations also took place using a 40-year-old decree allowing the government to 'requisition' enterprises that ceased production, failed to produce articles of basic necessity, or unjustifiably produced deficiencies in supply. Expropriation required full payment in cash and approval of an advisory board. This was used to take over a large textile mill idle since the election, and six other enterprises. Sometimes it was used to take temporary control, without payment;
- Similarly, Decree-Law 520 provided for intervention when there were labour disputes. When there were anti-government employer strikes in October 1972 and July-September 1973 the Decree-Law was invoked;
- There were also 'bottom-up' seizures by workers, including one after a day-long revolt by a tank regiment. Some enterprises seized this way were returned to the owners, as they were owned by friendly nations (Sweden and other European countries). In contrast to the nationalisation of US companies, there were no nationalisations of friendly European and Latin American companies.

Valuation, payment and source of finance

A constitutional amendment in July 1971 provided for copper-purchase compensation 'over a maximum of 30 years at no less than 3% interest on the basis of book value, less amortization, depreciation, fines, exhaustion of the mines, and reduced value due to obsolescence as well as all or part of the excess profits which those enterprises may have obtained.'[3]

The controller-general determined compensation on the basis of book value minus deductions as at December 1970. 'Excess profits' were left to Allende to determine. He began calculations from 1955, and took into account average profits of copper companies on a worldwide basis, the 1969 principle of higher taxation of profits received from higher copper prices, as well as other factors.

Allende announced excess profits as being over $770-million (all profits over 12% per year is the guess as to how he arrived at the figure). The controller issued his report of value minus deductions, and Anaconda was left *owing* Chile $78-million and Kennecott *owing* $310-million!

Allende's party justified his policy on excess profits, arguing that the copper companies should not receive compensation because they had already taken enormous profits from Chile. 'The act of nationalisation acquired the character of a penalty for the historical misbehaviour of the copper companies.' The official newspaper argued that 'a nationalisation programme not involving direct confrontation with the "imperialist" companies would lack any meaning, as it would not be the outcome of the struggle of the masses.'[4]

Compensation for share purchase by Corfo was paid in immediately negotiable certificates to the small shareholders, while large stockholders were to receive payments over two to seven years, depending on size.

The effects

Prior to the excess profits decision, the Allende government had been

> achieving impressive results in both the economic and political field. The government showed itself capable of initiating an extensive nationalisation programme as well as a generous policy of income redistribution, together with full employment and control of inflation. The initial economic policy brought about an industrial growth of nearly 12% and an increase of 8,3% in the GNP. The success of the economic policy was reflected in the successful electoral results in favour of the government in the municipal elections of April 1971.[5]

In November 1971 the new Chilean government refused to pay installments for the 1969 purchase of 51% of Anaconda. Kennecott sued Chile in the US courts and blocked the bank accounts of nine Chilean agencies. The order was rescinded in 1972 when Chile paid up, less $8-million for money 'not usefully invested'. More law suits followed in Germany, Belgium, France, Sweden, Italy and Holland. It took six years to finalise payments, made then by the new Pinochet military government. Internally, there was some notable resistance to the nationalisation programme. The largest private bank, Banco de Chile, offered to buy any shares that came on the market from a Fund for Liberty (collected from private contributions and also funded by the CIA).

Total nationalisations exceeded 500. In addition to copper, iron and steel, nitrate, telephones, electricity, the state sector included 30% of distribution, nearly all metal processing, soft-drinks, textiles, beer, cement, and much of construction.

Faundez argues that it was after the excess profits decision that the wheels came off. The multinationals and the US government attacked the principle of 'retroactive excess profits'. The Hickenlooper Amendment governed the US government's response to nationalisation of American companies. It did not oppose nationalisation in principle, but simply demanded that compensation be 'prompt' and 'fair'. On the basis that the compensation was not 'fair', the US government began to block all financial aid to Chile.

More seriously, the CIA and the White House began to organise a coup against Allende. The coup succeeded in 1973.

THE PERUVIAN EXPERIENCE, 1969-1976

A military coup in 1969 brought an 'enlightened' military government to power under President Velasco. The new government stressed that it recognised the rights of private property and foreign investment, but announced its decision to nationalise the International Petroleum Company (IPC). This followed an earlier court case where it was found that IPC had made profits from petroleum extracted illegally since 1924, valued at $690-million. The government offered to pay full compensation once this amount was settled.

Most IPC technicians were Peruvian, and most oil produced was consumed internally, making takeover easy. The only obstacles were the US government and the Hickenlooper and Sugar Acts to cut off provisions. While the US could not boycott the oil, it could cut off aid and access to international credit. After negotiations with the Nixon administration, it was agreed IPC would fight its case in the Peruvian courts. The US administration considered these actions to be 'appropriate steps', and a reason not to invoke Hickenlooper. By 1972 all IPC's assets had been nationalised, and all legal appeals had failed. The US then put an unofficial credit squeeze on Peru which lasted two years.

In a further move, the government expropriated coastal sugar estates owned by WR Grace. This was in line with land reform policies, necessitated because 2% of the rural population owned 90% of the land. Companies or corporations were forbidden from holding rural property, with a deadline of six months set for transferring the properties to rural co-operatives.

In 1969 foreign companies with copper mining concessions were ordered to file development plans or lose the concessions. Most plans filed were rejected, and concessions were cancelled without compensation. This action formed the basis for the creation of Mineroperu, which was given a monopoly over foreign mineral trading and domestic refining.

Part of the government's strategy was to develop a mixed economy: a state sector, a mixed sector, a private sector and a private reformed sector (to be the largest). The private reformed sector, based on the idea that each company form an Industrial Community (IC), was an innovative and ambitious scheme.

Each Community (company) was to distribute in wages 10% of annual profits and a further 15% in shares was to be held in the name of the workers. This would continue until worker ownership reached 50%, although the process could be delayed by additional investment by the owners. In fact a regular reinvestment of 30% of company profits was sufficient to prevent the IC ever gaining 50% ownership. But the ultimate aim was joint worker-management ownership of the IC. Foreign firms were also to sell majority control of their holdings to national investors over a fade-out period of 15 years. The Industrial Law thus set limits on new foreign investment, and divestment of existing investment.

In 1970 the government imposed exchange controls on the banking sector. It bought out banks owned by one of the 'big families', Chase Manhattan, and one another with American holdings.

In May 1973 the government announced all fishing companies would be nationalised and integrated into a single enterprise. The fish-meal market, an important source of foreign exchange, was collapsing at the time, and of 55 companies, only the American owned were likely to survive.

Valuation, payment and source of finance

By the time the military came to power it had already been agreed that ITT would be nationalised. The new government offered ITT $14,8-million (80% of book value) on condition ITT reinvested $8,2-million in a Sheraton Hotel and a telephone equipment factory. The company also obtained contracts to supply equipment and technical assistance.

Compensation for land nationalisation was set down in an agrarian Decree Law in 1969. It provided compensation bonds to land owners which could be used to finance up to 50% of new industrial investments if bondholders drew on other resources to finance the other 50%.

Compensation paid to Chase Manhattan Bank was three times book value and nearly six times the depressed market value! A friendly Chase was guaranteed.

Compensation in the fish-meal market was provided at book value with 10% paid in cash and the rest in 6% bonds over ten years. American companies involved rejected the valuations, and disputes erupted.

In 1973 Cerro, the largest American investor in Peru ($253-million) approached the Peruvian government to discuss nationalisation. But negotiations broke down over compensation, Peru offering $12-million and Cerro demanding between $175-million (book value) and $250-million (appraised value). Cerro withdrew its offer, but negotiations later resumed, and it was agreed that nationalisation would happen, and compensation worked out later along with other expropriation disputes. Peru increased its offer to $20-million. Personnel was retained and Cerro co-operation continued during this period.

It was notable that in Peru, no specific compensation was paid to US companies for many of the nationalisations: land, fishing, copper and others were expropriated without agreed compensation. Most of the proposed compensation was rejected by the US companies. Grace, for example, rejected the bonds as nearly worthless and the valuation of the company as too low. Instead an expropriation agreement was negotiated with the US government in 1974. A lump sum of $76-million was paid to the US government to distribute to the companies as it saw fit.

The Marcona nationalisation

The Marcona nationalisation of 1975, the final nationalisation undertaken by the Velasco government before it was overthrown in another military coup, is worth detailed mention. US-owned Marcona produced most of Peru's iron ore and was the last large mining company not nationalised. It produced iron ore in a liquid slurry form, and transported it with its own ships to markets in Japan, Germany and the US. Profits were enormous.

Velasco nationalised Marcona on several pretexts, but against the wishes of his minister of mines, who pointed out that 95% of the ore was exported, Peru did not have ships — or the capacity to replace the ships — and the ship transporters were designed specifically for the liquid slurry.

The iron ore industry collapsed. Marcona withdrew its specially-designed ships, which meant Peru could only transport the ore in leased ships not designed for the load. In addition, the world market for ore was weak. All of Marcona's customers withdrew. Japanese customers withdrew partly because the Japanese courts are very strict in imposing judicial sanctions on uncompensated expropriations. Iron exports thus dropped from five million tons (to Japan, the US and Germany) to 33 000 tons (to Rumania) in six months. The loss was $100-million annually, at a time when balance of payments problems were causing a grave financial crisis.

Compensation for Marcona was worked out only after Velasco was overthrown by a new military government, which offered $9-million, after deductions. Marcona wanted $167-million. The US government was asked to intervene and it was agreed that Marcona ships would start moving in the interim. Each side obtained valuators and the package was negotiated. Compensation, which in the end totalled $61,4-million, was to be

> a three part package that involved a $37-million promissory note to be financed by loans from a US banking group; $22,4-million from discounts to Marcona by Peru to be paid from the sale of 3,74-million tons of iron ore pellets over the next four years at a price set at $6-a-ton below the estimated future world market prices; and $2-million from the $1-a-ton payments under the December shipping contract.[6]

The effects

By 1970 foreign investment figures were negative and domestic investment dropped to half the rate of the early 1960s. Rationalisation in the fish market involved mass dismissals and union opposition.

Most important was a new coup by conservatives in the military in 1976, who dismantled what was termed Social Property. The fish industry was denationalised, nationalisations stopped, rural co-operatives were taken over by the government, the Industrial Communities were dismembered, and fade-out of foreign ownership ceased. Marcona remained nationalised.

In 1968 there were 12 state-owned companies. By 1976 there were 170 to 180 employing 120 000 people. The state controlled over 50% of the nation's capital formation. Between 1967 and 1973 public employees had grown from 270 000 to 410 000, and public debt grew from over $1-billion in 1969 to $5-billion in 1977. Domestic savings dropped from 16% of GNP in 1970 to 7,6% in 1976, and the percentage of investment financed by foreign borrowings rose from 2% in 1970 to 53% in 1975.

THE VENEZUELAN EXPERIENCE, 1974-1978

In Venezuela, nationalisation of the iron and petroleum industries was characterised by intense and detailed preparation. For example, the president's office held secret negotiations over five months with iron companies before reaching an agreement.

The oil nationalisation process went through the Venezuelan Congress, where it was necessary to develop a multiparty consensus. A presidential commission was established consisting of four ministers, the head of the state oil company, the chairmen of the petroleum committees of the congress and senate, a representative of the armed forces, a representative from each political party (of which there were eight), three labour representatives (including of the Petroleum Workers Union), three business and banking representatives, five representatives of universities, representatives from organisations of engineers, lawyers, economists and scientists, and five petroleum experts. The commission was divided into sub-committees covering operations, structure, finances, marketing and labour.

The terms of the commission were to develop an administrative formula for the transition to state ownership, and the resolution of problems involved in maintaining workers' benefits, and compensation. The commission established the following ground-rules for nationalisation of the oil companies:

- Workers be guaranteed their jobs and social benefits;
- Larger companies retain their operating identities, but their activities should be co-ordinated by a state holding company;
- The establishment of a guarantee fund equal to 10% of the gross accumulated investment of the companies;
- Compensation amounts be reviewed and approved by the supreme court;
- A complete state monopoly over exploration, refining, transportation and marketing.

Valuation, payment and source of finance

The iron companies had operated with 50-year concessions, which were rescinded by the government in 1974. A compensation package was worked out in three parts:

- A compensation payment, where the government provided for the payment of promissory notes at 7% interest over a period of ten years with the amount based on book value of all installations less depreciation;

- A one-year management service contract and three-year technical assistance contract with the two US steel companies under the supervision of the state steel company;
- Bethlehem Steel also signed a contract to purchase 3,3 million metric tons of iron a year, for three years, with a renewal option for two years, while USA Steel agreed to purchase 11 million metric tons a year over the next seven years.

In the case of oil the presidential commission decided that payment should be in bonds, the valuation calculated at net book value (cost minus depreciation and amortization) after deductions for taxes, worker benefits, property in deteriorated condition and 'drainage' from outside concession areas. Eventual compensation worked out to only 20% of actual investment and 10% of replacement value. But the valuation was based upon the oil companies' own books. Indirect compensation was built in, on condition they maintained a direct working relationship after an amicable settlement through payments for technical assistance and rights to purchase crude for company refineries. The companies were later billed for deficiencies in equipment and other assets, reducing compensation further by 15%.

Technical assistance was calculated per barrel. The more advanced the process (eg refined versus crude) the greater the technical assistance payment. The technical assistance agreement included loans of technicians, training, direct access to new technology, computer programmes, and assistance in the establishment of research capability. All but one of the US oil companies accepted the deal. The exception was a company involved in (unproven) bribery charges, and was not compensated at all.

In both the iron and oil cases company reluctance to accept compensation at book value minus depreciation was lessened by payments for technical and other assistance and Venezuelan production continued to find a large market in the US.

The US government claimed that book value as a basis of valuation was not adequate. It argued that payment should be calculated as a 'going concern' value. Nonetheless, the US government accepted the nationalisation, as there was no violation of international law and the entire process had gone through both the Venezuelan congress, the senate, and the courts.

The final agreement favoured the oil companies. They no longer operated the wells, took none of the risks, faced no labour problems. But their profits did not decrease commensurately — they continued to make as much as before nationalisation through favourable terms in technical assistance and marketing contracts. In fact, most of the increased profits earned over the period when they owned the oil fields disappeared in taxes. After nationalisation, revenue did not have to go back into new oil developments, but could be reinvested elsewhere in the economy.

By 1978 the government realised that it had erred in the terms of settlement. The technical assistance contracts were re-negotiated. Payments were calculated on technology man-hours rather than per-barrel produced or refined, sharply reducing these fees. The Venezuelan national oil company also developed its marketing arm, and decreased the amount of oil marketed by external companies.

THE BRITISH EXPERIENCE, 1945-1967

The 1945 Labour Government of Britain initiated a series of nationalisations: the Bank of England, coal, gas, electricity, iron and steel, transport and others. A minister of nationalisations was appointed.

Nationalising coal mines was a policy the Labour Party had advocated since 1919, and had been recommended by a commission under Churchill's conservative government. The motivations were partly to promote socialist aims and partly economic — to revive a flagging, out of date industry in desperate need of reorganisation and upon which the country depended for 90% of its energy.

The Coal Industry Nationalisation Act of 1947 gave the National Coal Board the responsibility to purchase, rearrange, organise and run the coal industry. It was decided to purchase the mines outright against opposition from the mineowners.

Nationalisation of electricity also occurred under the post-war Labour government through the Central Electricity Authority. As early as 1880 it was realised that electricity would be brought under government control. In the intervening years, the industry grew up as a combination of state and private companies, co-ordinated in a central grid system under government control. The Electricity Act of 1947 provided for the industry to be wholly nationalised. Despite opposition from private electricity supply and retail companies, nationalisation went ahead.

The gas industry, although older, faced similar problems. There were far too many inefficient operators, in firms of disparate size. Already, 36% of the industry was under government, mostly municipal, control varying in size and efficiency. Gas nationalisation was unopposed within the industry itself, although there was opposition in parliament. Control of gas supply remained local, although industrial relations and finance were co-ordinated through a national gas council. Unlike electricity many managers of gas operations remained. Several hundred gas works taken over were immediately shut down as part of the industry rationalisation.

The Transport Act of 1947 gave the Transport Commission the huge task of:

- Owning, controlling and reorganising the whole railway system, previously run by four major enterprises;
- Taking over 3 800 road-haulage undertakings and combining them into one public monopoly;

- Owning and running all passenger transport (road and rail) in Greater London;
- Reorganising passenger road transport for the rest of the country, some of which it already owned;
- Proposing schemes to reorganise harbours;
- Taking over all canals and docks, ships and hotels formerly owned by the railways, and acquiring the travel agent Thomas Cook.

Not all these tasks were carried through because of the change in government during the 1951 election, and also due to enormous resistance from private interests such as road hauliers. By 1951 the Transport Commission had acquired 3 766 road haulage undertakings. Fewer than 500 of these were voluntary sales. The 1951 Conservative government only left railways as a nationalised industry.

The Iron and Steel Act of 1949 set up an Iron and Steel Corporation which took over the securities of all the iron and steel companies in Britain — 298 concerns in all. By purchasing all shares of the companies the Corporation took over not only the steel-making plants, but also their subsidiaries, many of which were involved in engineering. The ISC left each operating company intact.

However, within eight months of the ISC beginning its work the Conservative Party was voted into power. In 1953 the new government began selling the companies back to private ownership. The share price slumped, however, because the Labour Party vowed it would re-nationalise the companies, and the companies were resold on very favourable terms. The Labour Party did re-nationalise the iron and steel companies in 1967. This time around it was more selective, nationalising only the largest companies and leaving intact a sizeable private sector. It undertook major reorganisation, removing any resemblance to the previous companies.

Valuation, payment and source of finance

The coal nationalisation was funded with stock issued by the government, not the National Coal Board. This stock was funded through annuities payable by the NCB over 50 years. Compensation totalled £388-million. The valuation of assets took until 1956, spreading the compensation payments over ten years.

Making the repayment period so long meant the repayments would be low. However, '50 years was far too long a period in relation to the life of the assets... They would be obsolete, if not physically worn out, at an early stage in the 50-year period. That in fact proved to be the case.'[7] In 20 years (by 1965) only 14% had been paid off. This left an outstanding debt to the government of £334-million, representing 300% of the written-down value of the assets. This debt was written off by the government of the day, transferring the burden onto the taxpayer.

With transport, gas, iron and steel and electricity no valuation had to be carried out. Compensation was paid purely on the basis of market value of the shares.

THE ITALIAN EXPERIENCE, 1935-1960

Rapid industrial expansion in Italy during World War One was financed by the Italian banks. After the war, however, the major banks experienced a liquidity crisis. To prevent the larger corporations from going bankrupt the Italian government intervened. A worsening economy by the 1930s prompted the Italian state to set up IRI (Institute for Industrial Reconstruction), which took over the three major banks

> in order to provide a unified management for the industrial securities the major banks had held. Thus, in response to domestic and international economic crises, the Italian government created a temporary state agency, IRI, to rescue the country's indebted firms.[8]

By 1939 IRI's share of total production included 70% of ship-building, 45% of steel, 39% of the electrical-mechanical and 23% of the mechanical engineering industry. Industries were nationalised only when they were in trouble, and needed a rescue operation; or when there was a request from the banks or businesses to have losses absorbed by the state. It has been described as the 'most casual nationalisation ever accomplished by a European country' and the result of continued rescue operations borne of the economic crisis rather than the product of fascist ideology.

It is interesting to note that while the fascist dictator, Benito Mussolini, initially referred to IRI as a clinic for firms temporarily in trouble, he later changed the policy, and IRI started to intervene more actively in the economy. State intervention carried on after the war as well. Opposition to state intervention was based on its being a 'remnant of fascism'. But the policy continued. In 1953 ENI (Ente Nazionale Idrocarburi), a state-owned enterprise in the oil and gas industry, was established as part of a conscious political strategy. It aimed to dismantle monopolies in the oil and electricity industries, then expand into telephones and related industries. This carried on into the 1960s.

FORMS OF ACQUISITION, COMPENSATION AND AGREEMENT

It has been argued that hostile seizure without compensation is not, in fact, nationalisation. When Iran nationalised Anglo-Iranian Oil in 1950, it refused to pay compensation. When the US was asked to mediate between Iran and Britain, Averell Harriman told the Iranian prime minister:

> In the view of the United States government the seizure by any government of foreign-owned assets without either prompt, adequate and effective compensation or alternative arrangements satisfactory to the former owners is, regardless of intent, *confiscation rather than nationalisation*. There must be more than a willingness to pay; there must be an ability to do so in an effective form.'[9]

The most accepted methods of nationalisation are those which result from negotiation — where there are negotiations with the company to be nationalised, and all parties agree to the terms. This method also gains acceptance with other companies fearful of nationalisation themselves.

In Latin America the few nationalisations accomplished without problems were those (notably ITT in Peru) where the company agreed to be nationalised and agreed to the terms of payment.

But the most usual situation is where the companies targetted do not agree to nationalisation. The nationalising government informs the company of the nationalisation, sometimes through the act rather than before it. The company to be nationalised usually objects and resists but cannot stop the process.

Case studies suggest that if it is not possible to negotiate nationalisation, the methods employed to effect the nationalisation, if sensitively handled, can smooth the way somewhat. Consultation with interested parties and experts, as happened in Venezuela, is one option.

This approach should not be under-estimated, particularly given the abilities of capital to relocate, banks to pull out, multinationals to withdraw, technology agreements to be rescinded, skills to leave, investors to withhold cash, and foreign governments to take punitive actions.

It does happen, though rarely, that a company requests nationalisation. This is largely how the government-owned Italian giant IRI was established. This usually occurs where the company has a profitability crisis, but is important to the overall economy and needs to survive in some form. This form of acquisition usually takes place with limited compensation, or none at all.

Taking over sick companies also has its problems. 'Hospitalisation gains the upper hand over rehabilitation.'[11] Management is less interested in pulling things right once the state and all its financial power is behind it. Thus what must be guarded against is institutionalising inefficiencies under recurrent public subsidy and developing permanent, complacent acceptance of the sickness.

Nationalisation *de novo*

One form of nationalisation which has not received much attention is *de novo* nationalisation. Public companies in developed countries have come into being mainly through nationalisation. In less-developed countries, however, they have been created *de novo* (from scratch) for the most part. Which is better?

On the one hand, scarce resources are not used up to pay for something which already exists in *de novo* nationalisation. On the other, a new company lacks the structures, management, financing, organisation and operation.

The road followed is often a function of the country's level of development. For example, in Britain and Italy, starting up public sector energy or broadcasting was easy because of the general level of technological development. In India it was more difficult. There most enterprises were started *de novo*, and most decisions relating to product-mix, capital expenditure, location and technology were new-venture incidentals.

In a review of large-scale nationalisations in Zambia, Tanzania, Somalia, Ethiopia, Egypt, Iraq, Bangladesh, Pakistan and others, it was concluded that different countries have shown similar errors. Advantages which could have been achieved at the operating and managerial levels

> have been overshadowed by organisational structures hastily created to take charge of the enterprise. They generally took the shape of giant apex bodies, within which were incorporated many similar...enterprises, unleashing a new series of costs — of over-centralisation in decision making. Large scale nationalisations have not been accompanied adequately by precise enunciations of the targets of performance sought for individual enterprises, unlike selective pieces of nationalisation.[10]

COMPENSATION

Most nationalisations take place soon after a new, often 'revolutionary' government comes to power. The nationalisation process itself tends to reflect a change in the power relations within the country concerned. So, too, does the compensation paid.

It is tempting for the new government to flex its muscles and pay no compensation, which would be popular amongst the electorate. There are many in the political left 'who believe that the amount paid as compensation is an indication of the revolutionary will of the government.'[11] Often this is accompanied by the desire for revenge for past ills, perceived or (in many cases) real.

At the other extreme of the compensation debate are those on the receiving end of nationalisation who argue that basic notions of fairness and justice demand market-related compensation. But not even the Hickenlooper and Sugar Act Amendments demand that compensation be at full market value, simply that it is fair, timely and effective. Compensation need not even be at 'going concern' value.

Green argues compensation turns on 'concepts of fairness — either of the decision-taking groups or of external bodies it cannot afford to ignore; questions of practicality usually directly or indirectly related to continued need for foreign markets, supplies, knowledge, personnel, and/or finance...'[12]

As in any takeover bid, the top limit is what the assets are worth to the new owner and the bottom is what the seller will accept. The bottom limit is special in this case since the seller cannot refuse to sell or find an alternative buyer. Unless there is unilateral price- setting the price that is ultimately set will be the product of negotiation.

'Fairness' thus becomes a crucial and debatable issue, depending more on notions in each country than on some internationally-accepted standard. In Britain 'fair' was market value; in Chile 'fair' was book value less deductions.

Six factors determine the accepted level of 'fairness' of compensation in a given situation:

- Acceptance of the fairness of private ownership and thus payment for expropriation;
- The historical context — claims for past injustices;
- Government's attitudes to specific class and racial groups, partly related to what is wanted from those groups;
- International opinion;
- Legal norms and protections;
- The view of ex-owners, and responses to fairness or unfairness.[13]

In Tanzania it was accepted that 'reducing an individual to poverty was not a fair result of nationalisation and that, by and large, ex-owners should receive about the book value of their net assets, unless they had engaged in gross exploitation.' The domestic aspects of fairness in Tanzania 'turned partly on value, partly on past actions of the owner, partly on public policy.'[14]

Compensation can take different forms and take place over different time horizons (Appendix 3.2). Table 4 summarises compensations paid in the case studies.

TABLE 4: Comparison of methods of nationalisation in selected countries

Nationalisation	Valuation Method	Payment Method	Interest	Pay Period	Additional Arrangements
Venezuelan Iron	Book Value (BV) less depreciation	Promissory notes	7%	10yrs	Management contract technical service & purchase agreement
Venezuelan Oil	Net BV (cost less depreciation amortisation and deductions)= 20% investment, 10% replacement value	Bonds		Agreement	Technical assistance – per barrel, then per hour; Purchase
British Coal	Full value — going concern	Gilt-edge stock		10yrs	
British Gas, transport, electricity iron & steel	Market value of shares	Gilt-edge government stock			Total value:£ 2 266m (1946-1951)
Mexican oil – Sinclair	Declared tax value (book)	Cash, discounts		3yrs 4yrs	Purchase agreement
Mexican oil – others	BV less deductions	Cash	Lump sum	5 yrs	
Cuba – land (unsettled)	Declared tax value (book)	Bonds	4.5%	20yrs	
Cuba – all other (unsettled)	Declared tax value (book)	Bonds	2%	30yrs	From fund of $ sales of sugar in US
Chile copper (Frei)	51% of book value & option on other 49%	Cash from mine profit	None	12 yrs	Retain management 3-year marketing contract – 1% of sales
Chile copper (Allende)	BV less amort, fines, depreciation & excess profit		3%	30yrs	(Mines ended up owing money to the government)
Chile – Corfo purchase of shares/companies	Full market share value	Negotiable certificate		Immediate – smallholders 2-7 years – large holders	
Peru – ITT	80% of book value	Cash		Immediate	(Reinvest 80% immediately); supply, technical assistance
Peru – land		Bonds			To reinvest
Peru – Chase Manhattan	3 x book value 6 x market value				
Peru – fish-meal	Book value	10%cash 90%bonds	6%	10yrs.	

VALUATION AND PAYMENT

Valuation itself is a complicated, and imprecise, process — more of an art than a science. Financial and accounting 'facts' are subject to interpretation, different assumptions about the present and future can be used, different accounting techniques produce different answers, and it is subjective since the seller always wants more and the buyer always wants to pay less.

If an attempt is made to be 'objective', then the value of a firm to a nationalising government is what the government can reasonably be expected to gain from the firm expressed in terms of the net present value of future benefits. These 'benefits' are usually income. There may be broader benefits such as creating employment, developing regional balance, providing markets for raw materials of other local firms, harnessing economies of scale, developing marketing strength, or improving the balance of payments position. These benefits must be discounted from the valuation because the present owner is not able to secure them for the firm.

The initial value placed on a firm is not necessarily the actual price paid. That is dependent upon the timing and period of payment, and the level of interest paid on the outstanding balance. If the interest rate is set above the going local or international bank borrowing rate, then this will not affect the price — the government will simply borrow the money to settle immediately. If, on the other hand, the interest rate is below the going bank rate then it will make the purchase cheaper for the nationalising government, and more expensive for the seller. This is only the case if there is an extended payment period, and this, combined with a lower-than-market interest rate on the balance, lowers the price of the purchase.

In Tanzania the standard agreement was for a downpayment of 20-30%, usually 15-24 months after acquisition because of the time required by negotiation — and the balance over 5-15 years, at around 6% per annum interest. The interest rate was about the rate of medium-term public debt in Tanzania. This phasing reduced the eventual cost of nationalisation. It also had two other advantages:

- For almost all acquisitions earnings from the investment exceeded compensation payments (except, of course, for the year of the downpayment);
- Compensation payments were exceeded by the profits which would have gone to foreign ex-owners, thus improving the balance of payments.

If it is important to keep management or technical services, marketing arrangements or purchasing facilities, this can be done through the ex-owner. Partial nationalisation or (relatively) agreed payment can wed the ex-owner to the firm. It may also be possible to nationalise outright and still secure services by management contract, alternatively replacement management can be hired or contracted.

If the ex-owner is tied to the company by a significant stake, then 'profit on that, plus management fees, are enough to ensure that the former 100% owner can be bargained down to a modest premium on book value, or five to seven years average recent post-tax profits.' This was used initially in Tanzania in the cigarette, can, cement, brewery and pyrethrum extract industries.[15]

> Nothing in such a first step prevents a subsequent 100% takeover when one is in a position to dispense with all or most of ex-owner's services... This implies a high degree of attention to...training clauses and/or a careful location of replacement management.

The purchase could be phased: an initial amount for a majority stake, then a phased purchase of the rest over several years, the price negotiated beforehand and tied to company performance after the initial state acquisition. To tie the ex-owner to the company, part of the compensation package could be connected to salary. This, in turn, could be dependent on reaching targets; or incentivised by tying compensation to performance. Compensation could also be tied to continuous operations, profit, skills transfer, and/or continued management, and technical or sales contracts. This is similar to arrangements reached during 'conventional' takeovers. (Appendix 3.2)

There are a diverse range of nationalisation processes which have been used — with different degrees of success. They range from the hostile seizure, usually conducted by a new government recently installed through a revolutionary process, to a negotiated nationalisation from an enterprise to a government which it trusts and upon which it relies. The range of different forms nationalisation can take is summarised in Table 5.[16]

TABLE 5: The options for different forms of nationalisation

Company	Agreement	Compensation	Option?
Whole	No	No	Confiscation
Part	No	No	Partial confiscation
Whole	No	Yes	Classic nationalisation
Part	No	Yes	Partial nationalisation
Whole	Yes	No	Not realistic
Part	Yes	No	Not realistic
Whole	Yes	Yes	Negotiated nationalisation
Part	Yes	Yes	Participatory nationalisation

There is an important, if obvious, distinction to be drawn from the above — that confiscation and nationalisation are not the same thing.

Outright confiscation is simplest to implement — in the short term. However, it usually results in a very hostile reception from the company being nationalised and from other countries, particularly if the confiscated company is owned by foreigners. In the longer term it creates the most complex effects, ranging from economic blockades to court cases and freezing of national assets in other countries.

If nationalisation is either negotiated or 'classic', then the entire issue of compensation must be taken into account. Calculating compensation is not straightforward. Each part of the package is open to negotiation or objection. The different parts include:

- The valuation method used;
- The method of payment used;
- The rate of interest used on outstanding balances;
- The period over which payment is made.

Each of these issues will determine the final price paid for the firm. Highly delicate, the outcome of the decisions taken will have an impact on the country's economy, notably on inflation and the balance of payments.

NOTES

1. Where not specified, information for the case studies in Latin America comes from: Sigmund, P, *Multinationals in Latin America: The Politics of Nationalisation*, University of Wisconsin Press, Wisconsin, 1980; and Ingram, GM, *Expropriation of US Property in South America: Nationalization of Oil and Copper Companies in Peru, Bolivia and Chile*, Praeger, New York, 1974; additional information on Chile from Faundez, J, 'A Decision Without A Strategy: Excess Profits in the Nationalisation of Copper in Chile', in Faundez, J, and Picciotto, S, (eds), *The Nationalisation of Multinationals in Peripheral Economies*, Macmillan, London, 1978. Information on British nationalisation is from Kelf-Cohen, R, British Nationalisation, 1945-1973, Macmillan, London, 1973; and Pryke, R, *Public Enterprise in Practice: The British Experience of Nationalisation Over Two Decades*, MacGibbon and Kee, London, 1971.
2. Sigmund, *Multinationals in Latin America*, p108.
3. Sigmund, *Multinationals in Latin America*, p150.
4. Faundez, *The Nationalisation of Multinationals in Peripheral Economies*, p92.
5. Faundez, *The Nationalisation of Multinationals in Peripheral Economies*, p90.
6. Sigmund, *Multinationals in Latin America*, p215.
7. Kelf-Cohen, *British Nationalisation, 1945-1973*, p26.
8. Martinelli, A, 'The Italian Experience: A Historical Perspective' in Vernon, R, and Aharoni, Y, *State-Owned Enterprise in the Western Economies*, Croom Helm, London, 1981, p87.
9. Quoted in White, G, *Nationalisation of Foreign Property*, Stevens & Sons, London, 1961, p184. (my emphasis)
10. Ramanadham, VV, *The Nature of Public Enterprise*, Croom Helm, Kent, 1984, p89.
11. Faundez, *The Nationalisation of Multinationals in Peripheral Economies*, p73.

12. Green, RH, 'A Guide to Acquisition and Initial Operation: Reflections from Tanzanian Experience 1967-74' in Faundez, J, and Picciotto, S, *The Nationalisation of Multinationals in Peripheral Economies*, p25.
13. Green, 'A Guide to Acquisition and Initial Operation: Reflections from Tanzanian Experience 1967-74', p25.
14. Green, 'A Guide to Acquisition and Initial Operation: Reflections from Tanzanian Experience 1967-74', p31.
15. Green, 'A Guide to Acquisition and Initial Operation: Reflections from Tanzanian Experience 1967-74', p34.
16. The designation of the form of nationalisation is not in current use — they are terms which are offered for ease of use and to distinguish between different forms of nationalisation. They are, in a sense, 'definitions' of nationalisation. The terms used will be described in detail within the South African context.

CHAPTER FOUR

NATIONALISATION IN SOUTH AFRICA

If there are to be nationalisations in South Africa, the shape they take, the valuations used, the compensation agreed upon, and the form of payment will have to be based upon South African conditions. Other countries offer valuable examples, useful lessons and indispensable guides, but the final resolution of this issue will be uniquely South African.

What form would nationalisation take in South Africa? Would a government simply pass legislation forcing private owners to give up ownership to the government, with or without compensation? Or would the minister of finance meet with targeted companies and reach an amicable, negotiated agreement?

What follows are some hypothetical considerations of practical (and impractical) options that might be applied in South Africa: what it would cost to buy certain companies, and how nationalisations could be financed.

FORMS OF ACQUISITION

There is only one sphere of the South African economy where nationalisation without compensation could seriously be proposed — the land.

Certain categories of land could be targets for confiscation — for example land occupied by white farmers after black resettlement, black spot land, or land owned by absentee landlords. In each case farmers, whether occupying or absentee, might simply lose ownership to the state, without compensation. Dolny, for example, seems to prefer confiscation to nationalisation:

> Farms owned by public companies and absentee landlords should, in principle, be nationalised... We may balk at the notion of compensation but the maintenance of production is important... The issue of compensation is double edged. The majority was once dispossessed by the minority in conditions of conquest. Blacks may claim for decades, even centuries of dispossession. Whites may claim the marketable value of the improved farmland...[1]

Dolny manages to avoid the 'double edge', recommending that compensation not be settled in the courts, but by a government commission. Owner- occupier farmers whose farms are the object of land claims, would then seek compensation from a National Land Fund through the commission. The National Land Fund would be based on a specific tax levied on all businesses, and those resources would be set aside from other state expenditure from the fund. In this scenario, land repossession could be immediate, with repayment connected to business profit and taxation.

But Dolny goes on, 'Many of the farms...actually have considerable bank debts. Thus the actual claims on the National Fund would be limited.'[2] The implication is that the land should be nationalised without inheriting the bank debts, effectively cancelling out compensation in many instances, and relieving the state of this burden in the nationalisation process. Neither the state nor the new farmer would be expected to take over the bank debt.

> The banks should write these off... Compensation to banks for such bad debts could be placed with a Compensation Commission which would have to weigh up the bank's claim against the manner in which the bank may have subscribed to over-extended borrowing.'[3]

The banks would thus pay the price for issuing the loan and failing to administer it properly. They, in the end, would finance the nationalisation. Through government commissions, present farmers would lose everything to the state which would then lease or sell the property to a new set of owners, leaving the banks a lot poorer and the new owners immeasurably richer. The state, in the end, would pay nothing.

While Dolny does not advocate confiscation, the form of nationalisation she proposes amounts to the same thing — neither the state nor the new owners/leaseholders pay for the property they receive.

Confiscation appears a cheap form of nationalisation, but its cost lies in the loss of tax revenue. Other probable negative effects include denting white farmer confidence and inducing capital flight. The latter may be limited because of the difficulty of converting fixed agricultural assets into liquid assets. White farmers trying to do this might precipitate a decline in land prices. If anything, this would enable the state to acquire other land at reduced cost, thus advancing redistribution programmes.

A fall in food production would be likely in the run-up to nationalisation. There would be increased 'soil mining' — the abuse of land to extract the maximum possible output in the short term, with a total disregard for soil conservation. The medium-term impact of this would be serious.[4]

Confiscation of land, or nationalisation without compensation, raises the possibility of economic dislocation and a decreasing supply of food for local and export consumption. Increased food prices have serious implications for the rate of inflation and the balance of payments.

Partial confiscation

Partial confiscation may be a means for the state to gain entry to large corporations which cannot be confiscated outright because their future viability then becomes uncertain. In other words, the government would not confiscate the entire company, but simply enough of its shares to obtain a large say in the running of the company's affairs.

Confiscation of assets is bound to engender resentment, resistance and fear both in the targeted company and the broader business community. As long as the prospect of total confiscation looms, owners and management may become demotivated and alienated, harming the company's long-term viability. Thus any such form of confiscation immediately creates antagonism between the partners, and any belief that management can be either convinced or disciplined to work effectively is definitely misplaced.

Classic, partial and negotiated nationalisation

Nationalising companies against the will of their owners, but with some form of compensation, is the most often cited form of possible nationalisation in South Africa. This method could be used to gain control over the commanding heights of the economy in general, and over monopoly corporations in particular. It is also applicable to those industries which are better placed under government control, and which are accountable to the public.

Cosatu, the ANC and the SACP base most of their arguments and proposals on this type of nationalisation, but stress that it is not 'an end in itself' and have modified the classic conceptions of nationalisation in their concept of 'socialisation'. However, socialisation, as we shall see in a later chapter, differs from classic nationalisation in the way in which it is implemented *after acquisition* rather than during acquisition.

Anglo American has already taken pre-emptive action against the possibility of classic nationalisation. While issuing fierce denials, the De Beers-Centenary listing effectively moved control of over 80% of De Beers' assets to Switzerland, making it almost nationalisation-proof. But the corporation has indicated it would be willing to enter into joint ventures with a future government.

Two forms of partial nationalisation are possibilities:

- The most common form, where the government purchases 51% of the shares in an enterprise; and
- Golden shares, where the government passes legislation requiring the company to restructure its capital to create a special category of shares owned by the state, giving the state a veto or effective control over company decisions. 'Such a "golden share" would represent a small proportion of the company's value. Obtaining it would involve low financial costs. But it would give the state key control over the enterprise's policy.'[5]

A third possibility offers itself because of the nature of capital formation in South Africa. The four largest corporations in South Africa control over 80% of all shares on the JSE, but directly own only 35%. It is through their controlling structures, reverse holdings, pyramiding and similar financial relationships that they are able to control so much. If even 51% of the correct 35% was obtained, the government could theoretically gain control of 80% of the JSE.

ANC deputy-president Nelson Mandela prefers the idea of negotiating nationalisation: 'We are very keen not to do anything without proper discussion with those interested and involved.'[6]

While no owner is likely to offer property for nationalisation voluntarily (particularly if compensation is not at market value), it is possible that once nationalisation becomes more of an option the largest conglomerates might come forward with proposals. This has a precedent in South Africa. When, in the 1940s, the new Nationalist government set up a commission into the possibility of nationalising Anglo American's mining interests, Anglo American itself suggested hiving off part of its interests to form a new company. The proposal was accepted, and General Mining was started. While General Mining did not become part of the state sector, it was sold off (at a low price) to the interests the government of the day wished to support. Tomorrow history may repeat itself — except this time the government might not wish the company to go to individuals but rather to itself.

Alternatively a future government, as in Venezuela, may approach the conglomerates, tell them of their intent to nationalise and ask them to make proposals. It is not inconceivable that the conglomerates would assent, albeit reluctantly.

It has already been mooted as a 'realistic possibility' that a future government and the large corporations negotiate a partial nationalisation of the conglomerates. The proposals vary. Management representatives say they are willing to consider models similar to the production councils of Germany where there is no direct ownership, but direct worker representation on the board; state representation on the board; or the state taking a direct ownership stake in the corporation, and receiving board representation commensurate with their stake so long as management is left with relative autonomy from political interference, and management prerogative remains intact.

This might form the basis for negotiated partial nationalisation, with compensation; or what might be called participatory nationalisation.

It is unlikely that companies will request nationalisation in the near future. The future government's nationalisation programme has not been spelled out, and present management trends in South Africa are towards privatisation and maintaining existing structures of power. However, requested nationalisation is possible, and could be successful — if the economic crisis continues and key industries begin experiencing crises in profitability. Under these circumstances it is possible South Africa might see its own version of Italy's IRI.

Economic crisis has already pushed the gold mines to request state assistance. Rand Mines' ERPM requested financial assistance from the present government. After a judicial commission the assistance was granted, with no strings attached. There is clearly a distinction between a request for assistance and a request for nationalisation. However, a repeat of the ERPM situation in the future might result in the government granting assistance but on condition that partial nationalisation takes place. In return for bailing out the mine, the government could demand control, or partial control, of the mine. Alternatively it could take a share in the controlling company.

FIXING COMPENSATION

Compensation to concerns being nationalised can be fixed in three ways:

- Market value;
- Book value;
- Book value less depreciation and other deductions.

Some have argued that it is impossible to have classic or negotiated nationalisation in South Africa at market value because it is simply too expensive. Let us take, as an example, the Freedom Charter's proposed nationalisation of the mines. The cost of classic and partial nationalisation calculated on the basis of the market value of these shares would be:[7]

TABLE 6: The cost of nationalising the mines at market value

Mining Sector	Classic Nationalisation	Partial (51%) Nationalisation
Coal	R 2-billion	R 1,0-billion
Gold	R 59-billion	R30,1-billion
Platinum	R 15-billion	R 7,7-billion
Diamond	R 23-billion	R11,7-billion
Sub-total	R 99-billion	R50,5-billion
Mining financials	R 76-billion	R38,8-billion
Total mining	R175-billion	R89,3-billion

Let us consider what it would cost to nationalise four companies: Rembrandt, Anglo American Corporation (AAC), SA Mutual and the SA National Life Assurance Company (Sanlam). Each of these companies merits study because of their different structures of ownership and control.

The Rembrandt Group Limited had a net asset value of R3 608-million in 1987. It is controlled by the Rembrandt Trust and the Rupert Family Trust through a controlling pyramid. Four of the companies in the pyramid are quoted on the JSE, the top three of which exist only to control 50% of the shares of the company below it, holding no other assets. The pyramid gives effective control to the Hertzog and Rupert families through holding only 8,6% — or R320-million worth of shares out of R3 608-million. Appendix 3.3 shows the pyramid and the asset value, while Appendix 3.4 shows what the pyramid controls.

Acquiring control over Rembrandt is comparatively simple and inexpensive. A nationalising government could gain total control of Rembrandt by buying, at full market value, the Rembrandt and Rupert Family Trusts for some R420-million. This is made possible by the pyramid-type control which the trusts have over the Rembrandt Group. The purchase could easily be financed from company earnings. This excludes Rembrandt's foreign interests controlled through Richemont.

The structure of Anglo American is very different. There is no pyramiding of control. Through direct ownership of only 8% of Anglo, via cross-holdings and nominee companies, the Oppenheimer family controls Anglo American and De

Beers. Part of the reason it can do this is because of the loyalty of the directors. The structure of Anglo American is shown in Appendix 3.5. As Riordan says:

> To purchase control of such a conglomerate is both immensely expensive and delicate. For the expropriation of the Oppenheimer shareholding...will not give you control in the face of hostility from the balance of the shareholders and directors. It is my belief that only by purchasing over 50% of the equity of the AAC, would a newcomer be assured of control.[8]

A share purchase of Anglo American in 1990 would cost R29-billion. Buying only 51% would cost R14,9-billion, which is more than the country's entire education budget.

Anglo American Gold (Amgold) has a market value of some R8,8-billion, giving 51% a value of R4,5-billion. This would purchase a minority stake in many of Anglo's mines (since they are held with a minority stake) which account for 40% of SA's gold output and 42% of the industry's pre-tax profit.

Anglo's 1990 net asset value (based on underlying asset values) is R37,8-billion. The value of the balance of the holdings is R42-billion, giving a total net asset value of R79,8-billion. An investment today of R19,3-billion (51%) would bring under state ownership and control assets of additional associated companies worth nearly R80-billion.

Anglo has a market-related book value per share of R57. Fifty-one percent of these shares (120 870 000) at a market related book value per share would cost R6,9-billion. The market value of Anglo American's shares in associated companies and general investments in 1990 was R40,5-billion. The non-market related book value of those shares was R4,12-billion and 51% of those shares would thus cost R2,1-billion. This would purchase ownership and control over 231 million shares generating attributable earnings after tax of R1,51-billion and equity accounted earnings after tax of R3,1-billion in 1990.

The market value of Amgold is R8,5-billion. It puts its book value at some R486-million. Thus, if book value of its investments is used as a basis of valuation control of over 40% of the nation's gold output could be purchased for R250-million.

Both SA Mutual and Sanlam are mutual life assurance companies. They are not held by JSE shareholders, but are rather 'owned' by millions of life policy holders and pension subscribers. SA Mutual has 1,3 million life policy holders and two million pension subscribers. Sanlam has two million policy holders. These policy holders do not, however, control the companies.

There are two possiblities for gaining control over Sanlam and SA Mutual. The first is to buy control from the policy holders. The value of policies under their control totalled nearly R40-billion in 1988. If 51% of each policy was bought by the state it would give ownership of these two groups, and control over vast assets that they control mainly through their investments on the JSE. Fifty-one percent would cost some R20-billion.

Valuation at book value is not a real alternative for the assurance companies since it is the value of the policies rather than an underlying asset value as represented in a share price that is being calculated. By the same token the mutual associations do not have shareholders who must be compensated. The government can simply appoint the top tier of management to act in the interests of the policy holders and the government. If the majority of policy holders support the government then this should not present a problem — it would, indeed, be possible to change the management not through legislation but through the popular will of the policy holders themselves.

Gaining control of these assurance giants could thus be cost-free, but would not be confiscation. Influence over a major asset base could be gained through the interests those companies hold on behalf of their policy holders. This asset base is outlined in Appendices 3.6 and 3.7. The range of potential purchase prices a nationalising government could offer is therefore wide. These are summarised in Table 7 below.

TABLE 7: Comparison of different purchase costs for select companies under full and partial (51 %) nationalisation

	FULL NATIONALISATION		PARTIAL NATIONALISATION	
	Market Value (R mil)	**Book Value (R mil)**	**Market Value (R mil)**	**Book Value (R mil)**
Rembrandt	4 873	not available	2 500	not available
Rembrandt-controlling Trusts	420	* 377	210	* 190
Anglo American	37 800	* 13 500	19 300	* 6 900
Anglo shares in associated co's	40 500	4 120	20 700	2 100
Anglo Am. Gold	8 500	490	4 300	250
JCI	7 100	1 500	3 600	770
Gold Fields	7 700	1 390	3 900	710
Old Mutual and Sanlam	40 000	not applicable	20 400	not applicable

* Book value of assets not supplied in the Annual Financial Statements. Valuation is not book value of assets, but market-related book value of shares.

Computed by:

$$\text{Book value per share} = \frac{\text{Common stockholders' equity}}{\text{Number of common shares outstanding}}$$

PAYMENT

The form of payment, the period over which it is paid and the interest paid on outstanding balances also determines the eventual net worth of the payment.

For example, an immediate cash payment of R100-million could be agreed on for a company. Alternatively the decision could be to pay R50-million cash immediately, and the other R50-million in R10-million installments over the next five years. While the amount paid is still R100-million, the effects of inflation mean the R10-million paid in year five is worth a lot less than in year one. The net present value would be less for the second form of payment than the first — favouring the buyer rather than the seller. If an interest payment is then calculated in on the outstanding balance each year, so long as it is at market rates, no-one loses. The seller gains if it is above that rate and the buyer gains if it is below.

These decisions can also affect the ease of payment and the impact of the payment on the nationalising government, the company and the economy as a whole. Some of the combinations of these decisions are summarised in Table 8.

TABLE 8: Some options for the time period, form of payment and source of finance for nationalisation

Time period	Form of payment	Source of finance
A. Immediate	1.Cash — local currency	Government: i. Printing money, ii. Existing savings, iii. Tax
	2. Cash — foreign currency	Government: reserves
	3. Equity	Government: stake in that or other company
	4. Debt	Company or government.
B. Deferred: 2-30 years	1. Standard interest-bearing bonds	i .Government issued ii. Company or government payments of interest and capital
	2. Two-tier bonds according to size of holding	i. Government issued ii. Government or company payments
	3. Annual cash payments	i. Company: dividend from profits, under-written by government.
C. Deferred/ Indirect	1. Marketing agreements 2. Management contracts 3. Technical agreements	Company revenues and working costs
D. Combinations	Combinations	Government and company

Immediate payment in cash

Payment in cash — either in local or foreign currency — is an extremely expensive form of finance. It raises the effective cost of the purchase (which could of course be calculated down to compensate). More seriously, it is likely to be inflationary.

Payment in foreign exchange affects foreign currency reserves. A large drain of foreign currency depresses the value of the Rand, pushing up import costs and adding to inflation. It is most likely that owners would want payment in foreign exchange, but it is also highly unlikely their wishes would be granted. Payment in local currency impacts in two ways:

- If payment is from current tax revenue or existing government savings there would be a substantial opportunity cost associated with the payment — the government thereby gives up the opportunity to spend this money elsewhere. Given the likely speeding-up of government spending on social and economic projects to overcome the problems associated with apartheid, it is unlikely this opportunity cost would be accepted.
- If money is printed to cover the cost, inflation will be substantially increased.

Whether payment out of current revenue or savings fuels inflation depends on what the recipients do with the money. If they leave the money in the bank this will have a positive effect, bringing down inflation by increasing the proportion of savings and decreasing the money in circulation. But it will also decrease the amount of money available for reinvestment, depressing growth in the longer term.

It is possible for the government to agree to immediate payment from tax revenue or its own savings should the money be reinvested in projects the government favours. While this would get around the potential for inflationary effects or depressing growth, it would not result in any net change in income and wealth distribution. It would simply have changed those private sector holdings from one part of the economy to another. Whether this is acceptable or not depends upon the aims of that particular nationalisation — if it was simply to get control of a key sector of the economy and not to achieve any redistribution, then it would be acceptable.

The only positive motivation for this form of payment would be to minimise potential opposition to nationalisation — and for the payment to be seen as immediate and fair. On balance, a nationalising government is unlikely to see many benefits to immediate payments in local currency, and even fewer in foreign currency. What is probable is immediate payment of a small portion of the total in local currency, as part of a package using a combination of types of payment outlined in Table 7. This form of combination payment has been used in most nationalisations.

Payment in equity

Payment in equity (or shares) can take different forms. Ex-owners could see their enterprise partially nationalised, leaving a substantial stake under their control. This would tie them to the firm, as well as decrease compensation payments since only part of the total value of the firm or asset needs to be paid. The equity stake is not a payment as such, but it does serve partly as compensation payment — the stakeholder now receives a portion of future profits.

If the programme of nationalisation is accompanied by a general review of government holdings, then privatisations may be occurring at the same time. The companies or assets being privatised could be part of an 'equity swop', should the ex-owner of the nationalised industry be so inclined.

In a further option, the ex-owner could be offered part equity in government-controlled companies. While this is not usual, it might be used where expertise and management skill is needed and only an equity stake would entice it.

A fourth method could be a partial re-privatisation of the nationalised company. The new state-owned firm could immediately issue stock on the JSE to raise funds either for payment of the original purchase, or to finance investment. However, it is unlikely that the market would initially value such stock very highly. In addition, it would be difficult to see who would buy it. Harris argues against issuing new stock to finance investment, given the present structure of the stock market:

> The Stock Exchange today has two characteristics that make it unsuitable: one is that it is overwhelmingly dominated by shares issued by Anglo American, a few other monopolies, and their subsidiaries; the other is that it is oriented toward trading and speculating in existing shares rather than the provision of new finance for the industry.[9]

If this argument holds, then issuing new shares to finance the purchase (a partial re-privatisation) would not be advisable.

Payment using debt

It has been suggested that debt would be a good means to raise the capital necessary for large-scale redistribution of land through nationalisation. If compensation is paid in cash the state would have to borrow, as its capacity to fund payments out of current state revenue is very limited. Interest and capital payments could in theory be paid for by the recipients of land, but it is improbable.

Debt can be either internally or externally generated. Harris advocates internal borrowing, and not only from banks. 'The state should borrow from the masses by creating such a range of new saving instruments itself rather than relying on the banks and building societies to offer them new forms of deposits.'[10] Presumably existing savings institutions such as the post office savings bank could be used for this purpose. But this is optimistic. The need is enormous and the level of domestic saving pitiful. It will take many years before the 'masses' can generate enough personal income to live above subsistence levels, let alone generate savings.

Debt should be considered as a source of compensation payment if normal commercial considerations can be shown to apply: primarily if returns on debt exceed the interest payment, but also if the extent of leverage does not exceed levels which normally characterise the industry (if a conservative borrowing policy is used); if it helps maximise the generation of wealth; and if the opportunity costs associated with it can be justified.

Paying with bonds

Paying with bonds may take different forms and several considerations have to be taken into account:

- The face value of the bond;
- The yield to maturity (how many years to final payment);
- The interest on the outstanding balance;
- Interest payment policy.

For example, one million Bond 'A's could be issued with a value of R100 each to cover compensation of R100-million. The bonds would be issued for 20 years and pay an interest of 10% per annum in two installments every six months. Bond 'B' could also be issued in R100 lots totaling R100-million, for ten years and pay an interest of 6% per annum. The possibilities are infinite.

Normally, bonds can be traded. In this way a market in compensation bonds could develop, with (perhaps) Bond 'B' being more highly valued than Bond 'A' despite the lower interest it offers, because there is a shorter time to maturity (ten years). This would reflect market belief that there is less risk in the face value of the bond being paid within the shorter time period. Anyone could purchase the bonds, but the most likely purchasers would be large financial institutions. If tradable bonds are used to finance compensation, the recipients of the bonds would be able to sell them immediately to realise the face value (or as near as possible, depending on the discount rate the market mechanism sets). This would, in effect, work as a cash payment, financed by the purchasers of the bonds, and guaranteed by the government that issued the bonds.

The arguments against using tradable bonds as compensation are similar to those against cash compensation.This is because bonds are in effect cash payments, with the same inflationary effects.This gives the ex-owners the ability to turn their assets, converted to cash through nationalisation, back into assets. Thus there are arguments for using non-tradable bonds as compensation. If ex-owners could not immediately sell the bonds for cash their assets would have been converted from ownership of enterprises to loans to the state on which they receive interest.

The necessity for such restrictions on sale are questionable. If there are large bond issues, there would not necessarily be a market for the bonds because of the enormous quantity of bonds that would be marketable. Given the proliferation of bonds, and the riskiness that would inevitably be attached to them after nationalisation, the market would discount them enormously. There would ultimately be a market level at which they could be sold, even at substantial discount. If this was the case, it would pay the government to buy back the bonds and finance the purchase through long-term borrowings. But the market is unlikely to reach such levels, as the bond-holders would be more content with holding onto the bonds, and receiving interest, than selling at a very low price.

The implication, in the South African context, is that when negotiations over the form of payment for nationalised industries take place, it is likely ex-owners will demand a high interest rate attached to the bond. This could put severe stress on the nationalised company which would pay the interest (either directly or through the government). Between 1945 and 1951 the British Labour Party used bonds as compensation

> and an active financial policy attempted to keep interest rates in general low initially so that the owners received low yields on the bonds. This method avoids some of the costs of other forms of compensation but the new bond issue will have an impact on the country's whole system of finance (and on the accounts and management rules of the nationalised industries) which will have to be taken into account.[11]

If a South African government aims to keep interest rates down for low yields on the bonds, it will have to be cautious. The ability to do this will depend on bringing the inflation rate down as well. High inflation and low interest rates — a real rate that is negative — means no private or corporate savings incentive. This may be fundamental to the opening up of new places for investment, developing the mass consumption markets, and so on.

A bond issue is not a simple form of payment in nationalisation of a company. It is, however, one of the most straight-forward methods and is favoured where the bond can be issued at a face value, over a period, and at a rate which is clearly in favour of the purchaser.

A tiered bond can also be issued. This form of bond would be used in cases where a company's shares were held by a cross-section of investors which a nationalising government wished to compensate differently. For example, in the case of Anglo American Corporation a cross-section of share owners may be:

- The Oppenheimer family, with each person worth hundreds of millions of Rands;
- Directors, who have received enormous directors' fees, and own blocks of Anglo shares worth millions;
- Foreign investors;
- Other large conglomerates such as Barlows;
- Pension funds, insurance and other companies and funds which invest on behalf of individual policy holders;
- Employee share holders participating in Anglo's ESOP (Employee Share Ownership Programme);
- Small individual investors;
- 'Widows and orphans' — people who depend on that dividend income for their survival, or who depend on capital appreciation for their long-term security. In fact the 'small investor' has nearly disappeared from participation in the JSE, holding only 1,4% of all shares.

It is possible to compensate each of these groups of shareholders differently. Those, like the Oppenheimers, who have already received millions from their interests and would not in any way be impoverished by a low rate of compensation for their shares, could receive a low-yield bond. This would trade at a large discount if sold on the market. Others, like the 'widows and orphans' could receive a high-yield bond which is easily tradable should they wish to realise their capital investment immediately, or which could continue paying a secure and definite interest year after year. Pension funds could receive a third rate, and so on. The point is that the bonds could be designed to pay compensation commensurate with concepts of fairness, and take into account the potential impact of nationalisation on the shareholders concerned (and, indeed, on the entire economy).

Annual cash, indirect or deferred payments

Annual cash payments are similar to bond payments, except that they do not go through the government, and are directed from the nationalised company to the ex-owner. This is, in effect, an annual dividend, normally financed out of company profits. But,

> the distribution of company profits as dividends may reduce the country's total savings. It reduces corporate sector saving and, if the dividends are paid to individuals, is likely to lead them to have higher consumption levels than they would if profits were retained in the company.[12]

It is also questionable whether companies will be able to generate sufficient profits to cover reinvestment needs as well as the large debt burden of compensation.

Only 1,8 cents in every Rand passing through 347 listed companies went to shareholders in 1990. On turnover of R207-billion dividends came to R3,6-billion; labour received R60-billion; and R5,3-billion was paid in tax. Profits before tax were R18,77-billion (9% of sales). In the mining sector the payout was higher with 12,4 cents in every Rand of sales going to dividends in 1988.[13]

Dividend payments could be used as the basis for calculating the kind of annual compensation payment these corporations could cover out of generated profits. It is assumed:

- Profitability does not decline;
- Tax revenue to the state should not be decreased — otherwise state spending on social and economic necessities would have to be decreased;
- Retained earnings should not pay for compensation as this would seriously jeopardise the long-term strength and viability of the company. For example, the gold mines are planning to spend R30-billion in 1990-1994 on new ventures, capital projects and improvements. This expansion programme should not be stopped to provide for compensation payments;
- There will be classic 100% nationalisation, leaving no other shareholders to compensate in dividends;
- The dividend payments simply cover the interest on the bond rather than the capital amount.

On this basis we can calculate the size of bond the dividend payments could service at different interest rates for various firms. (The calculation is laid out in Appendix 3.8)

Dividends could easily be used as a source of finance to cover completely the purchase of the Rembrandt controlling trusts (value: R377-million for full nationalisation at market-related book value of the shares), if other shareholders were to take lower dividends for a (brief) period. The dividends would not, however, begin to cover even the interest payments on a market value purchase (value: R4 873-million for full nationalisation).

A full nationalisation of AAC at market-related value would cost R37,8-billion; at book value of the shares the amount would be R13,5-billion. Using the full dividend payout would not even cover half the interest payments at 12% interest on this book value.

A full nationalisation of Amgold at market-related value will cost R8,5-billion; and at book value R490-million. Using the full dividend payout of R275-million per annum will comfortably cover both the interest and capital amounts of a purchase at book value in five years.

A full nationalisation of JCI at market-related value will cost R7,1-billion; and at book value R1,5-billion. Using the full dividend payout of R160-million per annum will almost cover the interest payments on a book value nationalisation — but only at a low rate of interest.

Thus, in certain circumstances it is feasible to pay for the compensation arising out of full nationalisation, including the capital amount and interest. In others, dividends could be used to cover interest only. However, there are cases where dividends generated are not nearly enough to cover even the interest bill on a full nationalisation at book value. In these cases compensation payments would have to be funded by sources outside the company.

In the case of indirect and deferred payments the costs of marketing agreements, management contracts, and technical agreements would effectively be covered by company income, and incorporated as part of company working costs. They should, of course, only be considered where they will be directly reflected in profits for the company.

In South Africa this might be an important form of compensation given many companies' dependence on the skills and knowledge of a very few people. The top tier of management, which participates in share ownership schemes in the company to be nationalised, can be offered compensation through participation.

THE POTENTIAL EFFECTS OF NATIONALISATION

Critics in the business sector predict that nationalisation will precipitate a crisis of confidence, a brain drain, capital flight, an end to foreign investment, a crash in the Johannesburg Stock Exchange and, finally, economic collapse.

A nationalising government would have to evaluate whether this is power-playing or sober assessment. For example, Anglo American might not take kindly to nationalisation of its gold interests, but if its directors were assured that this was as far as nationalisation would go, they might not complain too bitterly. They would be compensated, still retain massive interests in JSE stock, and might even feel that they 'got off lightly'. It would not be in their interests to precipitate a JSE collapse or a brain drain.

A future government might decide there is a high risk of negative reaction no matter how delicately the nationalisation process is handled. In that case it should do a cost-benefit analysis: Would the nationalisations be worth it? Would what is gained in strategic ownership be outweighed by the loss in capital or skills? Would the JSE be severely or marginally damaged?

This all-or-nothing mathematics — provoked by business' over-reaction on the one hand and government bravado on the other — is dangerous. It is also unnecessary. It is better to understand the roots of the potential crisis of confidence.

A crisis of confidence would be based on the belief that nationalisation is bad for the economy — that the new government's economic programme was unworkable and destructive, and that widespread nationalisation would be bad for individuals, leading to loss of property, value and income.

Assuming the ANC makes up the government of the near future in South Africa, a brain drain in response to nationalisations would remove skills necessary to make nationalisation work. There are not enough people in the ANC skilled in management, not enough — if any — members of the present civil service who would participate in nationalised structures with any enthusiasm, and not enough executives and trained personnel sympathetic to the aims of nationalisation.

Initially, all the ANC's best personnel would go into running the government and the vast bureaucracy, leaving few to staff newly-nationalised industry. While there are many unionised and pro-ANC people in industry, they are mostly at lower less-skilled levels, unable even collectively to run complicated industries.

In this context the loss of key management would threaten the very survival of these companies.

Even if the management remains, some claim the organisational culture binding the companies together would be so severely knocked by a forced transition to nationalisation, that it might precipitate their collapse. Who then would suffer most?

- Those who might leave the nationalised industry for another firm include managers, skilled personnel (engineers, accountants, marketing and salespeople) and consultants.
- There are also those who might leave the country: owners of industry, smaller entrepreneurs, managers, professionals such as doctors and lawyers, skilled graduates such as engineers and accountants — people who are the present major beneficiaries of the apartheid-based economy.

Both groups would be a great loss to any new government and economic structure. Their skills are not immediately replaceable.

- The holders of capital can be broken down into four main groups: foreign capital which remains invested in South Africa despite sanctions campaigns; foreign capital which might reinvest or newly invest in an apartheid-free economy; South African companies; and rich South African individuals.

● Investors in the stock exchange are dominated by large corporations and financial institutions. The turnover of shares in any one year is less than 5% of the total value of shares. One of the reasons is that, quite simply, there are few sellers and few buyers. Will these corporations and institutions panic in the face of nationalisation? If they sell *en masse* a collapse will happen. In that case the only buyer will be the state, and it may wait until prices reach rock bottom before buying.

Precipitating the crisis of confidence?

The impact on confidence will be primarily determined by the extent and type of nationalisation — confiscation, classic, partial, negotiated.

Many of the impending-doom statements from business are based on the fear of wholesale confiscation or large-scale, partially compensated nationalisation. These options, they say, will definitely lead to collapse and flight. But confiscation and large-scale nationalisations are highly unlikely.

A more interesting question is whether classic or partial nationalisation would also have a devastating effect on the economy. In most countries business community response has been conditioned by four factors:

- The context of the nationalisations;
- The extent of compensation, and perceptions of its fairness and effectiveness;
- The method of nationalisation — whether it goes through parliament and the courts;
- The response of the international community.

If nationalisation is perceived as an anti-capitalist assertion of working-class muscle it would hardly be surprising if capitalists experience a crisis of confidence and cut and ran. If, however, nationalisation is part of an overall, workable economic plan in the interests of a broad range of the population, there may merely be doubts, possibly even an attitude of 'wait and see'.[14] By the same token if the nationalisation appears dictatorial or unfair the effects on confidence would be negative. If nationalisation is used as a well-honed economic weapon, and not as an indiscriminate bomb, it may win favour.

THERE ARE WORKABLE METHODS OF NATIONALISATION

Confiscation and partial confiscation are undesirable. These methods applied in other parts of the world have antagonised suppliers, customers, owners, foreign governments and parts of the local population. In some cases the outcome has been the government's downfall. In others the result has been economic isolation.

Nationalisation *de novo* is expensive — but is not contentious and is feasible.

Classic and partial nationalisation, favoured options among South African proponents, could give control to the government, depending upon the structure of the company. If it were a pyramid structure (such as Rembrandt) a very partial nationalisation would gain complete control.

Participatory nationalisation might well be considered by business. However, the terms on which the private sector would negotiate would be unlikely to be supported by the government, and vice-versa. There would be difficulties, too, in negotiating restructuring proposals.

Negotiated nationalisation is the method which the ANC seems to prefer. At this stage there is too much emotion in the debate to be able to say conclusively whether it is either a possibility or an impossibility. If nationalisation *is* to be pursued this should be the first method explored by the government.

Nationalisation is affordable

Fixing compensation is a complicated process involving the two major valuations at market value and book value. Variations of these have been used successfully elsewhere.

Nationalisation as suggested in the Freedom Charter is too expensive, no matter the valuation techniques used. However, if these are kept as very long-term goals, they might become possible. But whether these goals are desirable has already been questioned by Charterists themselves.

Until recently the debate in South Africa has considered two options: no compensation at all (confiscation) or full market value. Full market value — the exception in nationalisations around the world — makes nationalisation prohibitively expensive in South Africa. The cost of nationalising Anglo American or any of the other major conglomerates in South Africa is not feasible at market value — unless it is a partial nationalisation of the controlling interests where pyramiding has occurred. If nationalisation at full market value were proposed for pyramid structures, another issue arises: it is likely the value of the remaining shares will decline after the government takes control of the pyramid. If the government extends the offer to remaining shareholders, they may sell their shares at market value (in which case it might become too expensive to nationalise). However, if the government simply takes control of the pyramid (at market value), and the other shares decline in value, then the non- controlling shareholders lose out. Either the minority shareholders are compensated in some form for this loss in value, or the government accepts an iniquitous situation where the large shareholders end up receiving full market value for their shares, while everyone else suffers losses.

One method of valuation can be based upon what the companies themselves say they are worth. The declared value for taxation purposes is the book value of the company. Using this valuation system:

- All Anglo American's shares in associated companies could be bought for a little over R4-billion;
- A controlling share in Rembrandt would cost R377-million;
- Anglo American Gold could be bought for under R500-million;
- JCI could be bought for R1,5-billion;
- Gold Fields for R1,4-billion; and
- Majority control over the whole of Anglo would cost in the region of R6-billion.

Fixing compensation at book value makes nationalisations of most companies realistic. The exception is the insurance and pension fund giants (Sanlam and SA Mutual) which have a corporate structure and identity not conducive to book value measurements. However, compensation at book value is likely to be rejected by major company shareholders, who would see this method as unfair.

Other methods of valuation have been successfully used in negotiated nationalisations using book value minus deductions. There are, again, arguments to back this valuation.

For some, like Rembrandt, market value of shares can be paid. In other cases book value or book value minus deductions can be used. A nationalising government must decide whether each nationalisation should be treated as a separate case, or whether a single valuation formula should be applied to all cases. It must bear in mind that compensation will probably be negotiated with the owners involved, and that this is likely to be a key sticking area.

While the owners are sure to complain about non-market formulae, the final settlements are likely to be large enough for them to live well for generations. Even a book value minus deductions settlement would leave Anglo American directors with millions, and the Oppenheimer family with hundreds of millions in the bank.

Whichever valuation is used, there is likely to be dispute. Valuation techniques themselves are disputable, since they are not objective and scientific. This means that fixing compensation would have to be a process negotiated between the buyer and the (forced or voluntary) seller.

Source of finance for compensation

The timing, form of payment and interest paid affect the eventual cost of nationalisation. That must be factored in during any negotiations or offer.

The form of payment most favourable to the seller is foreign currency cash. For the buyer (the government) it is payment in low-yield, tiered, non-negotiable bonds. The government can, to a large extent, determine the form payment takes — so it is more likely to be the non-negotiable bond. Foreign currency payments are almost inconceivable.

Other forms of payment to be considered include deferred payments such as management contracts, marketing and technical agreements, and combinations of different forms of payment. The aim here would be to encourage management expertise to remain with the company. This is particularly important in the context of a skills shortage.

Ideally, the value placed on the company and the form of payment negotiated should be related to company performance and its ability to generate the funds needed to meet the compensation payments. If this is not the case, compensation payments will serve as a drain on the treasury. This would then enter the calculation of affordability. The case studies of Anglo American, Rembrandt and others have shown different abilities to meet payments from profits. If the state cannot finance compensation payments, and if compensation cannot be favourably negotiated, there are two possible options:

- The state suspends all negotiations and unilaterally imposes a settlement. This could be done in the event of particularly unreasonable demands, such as compensation based on market value plus goodwill;
- The nationalisation itself is suspended.

However, these factors should not arise if this issue has been considered in the targeting process. Looking at profit figures of possible target companies could show that in most cases they would not generate sufficient profits to cover compensation payments. Depending on the valuation used for compensation, some will not even generate sufficient funds to pay the interest on the bonds. In this situation there would be reverse gearing and the government would have to fund the takeovers. Through combinations of different sources of financing, and if valuation methods which lower the cost of compensation are agreed to, then it is possible to finance nationalisation of large corporations.

It is possible to pay different degrees of compensation within the agreed valuation system to different shareholders. Those who could show that hardship would be induced by the nationalisation ('widows and orphans') or investors who would be severely affected (unit trusts and assurance companies) could be paid out on a different tier to those who would suffer no hardship at all.

Valuation, compensation and payment are highly contentious issues in the nationalisation process. Owners aim to obtain the greatest possible compensation, while the buyer — in this case the state — wants to pay as little compensation as possible. If the government does not wish to alienate a powerful, if small, section of the population, it will have to enter into debate over fair compensation.

A unique formula

Several interesting distinctions arise when comparing South Africa to other countries. In Ghana, Tanzania and Latin America compensation was paid to foreign owners. Mobilising local sentiment made it possible to target any foreign company for nationalisation, with few local repercussions. Debates about fair compensation depended on the colonial or neo-colonial track record of the company. In most instances the local population supported low valuation and terms of compensation favourable to the nationalising government. There was little the foreign company could do to stop the process, although they could withdraw their co-operation.

In South Africa the reverse is true — for the most part the companies which are potential targets for nationalisation are owned and controlled by South Africans. In certain cases local ownership is very broad.

Given that company owners live and work here, and are integral to the companies on a daily basis, it is not as easy for a nationalising government to fix fair compensation at low levels and pay on terms transparently unfavourable to the ex-owners. Book value compensation in bonds at low rates of interest would produce a specifically local reaction — not a foreign-engineered coup in the manner of Allende's Chile!

In Britain, of course, it was not foreign companies that were nationalised. There full market value was paid to local shareholders, making it easier for the Labour Party to win acceptance of its policy. However, in Britain's case the exchequer was strong and large enough to finance such massive purchases. The government could afford to write off debts of hundreds of millions of Pounds. The South African treasury is not in such a fortunate position. Nationalising at full market value is not an option, and allowing such huge debts to be written off would be impossible, particularly for a treasury financing post-apartheid reconstruction.

If compensation was minimal the effect would be negative — at a time when a new national unity is most needed. If it was market related then there would be large implications for state spending or borrowing.

What is certain is that there will be a large-scale diversion of funds to pay for compensation. Questions to be asked then are: Is it worth it? Is there the money? What are the opportunity costs of such a purchase? Would the gain outweigh the payment? Can this be justified, with all the financial implications? Is the nationalisation worth the price?

NOTES

1. Dolny, H, 'Agriculture: Conflicts of Interest in A Mixed Economy', paper prepared for the ANC-Cosatu Conference on the Post-Apartheid Economy, Harare, April 1990, p17.
2. Dolny, 'Agriculture: Conflicts of Interest in A Mixed Economy', p18.
3. Dolny, 'Agriculture: Conflicts of Interest in A Mixed Economy', p18.
4. De Klerk, M, 'Restructuring The Rural Economy: Agricultural Economic Aspects', unpublished working paper for the 'Rural Land' workshop of The Institute For Democratic Alternatives in South Africa (Idasa), 1989.
5. Harris, L, 'The Mixed Economy of A Democratic South Africa', paper delivered at the Lausanne Colloquium of the Institute for Social Development, University of the Western Cape, as part of the Research Programme of Economic Research on South Africa (Erosa), Switzerland, 1989, p10.
6. *Business Day*, 21/2/90.
7. Adapted from *Financial Mail*, 16/2/90.
8. Riordan, R, 'The Nationalisation of Industry in South Africa', in *Monitor*, April 1990, p107.
9. Harris, L, 'Building the Mixed Economy', paper prepared for the ANC-Cosatu Conference on the Post-Apartheid Economy, Harare, April 1990, p8.
10. Harris, 'Building the Mixed Economy', p7.
11. Harris, 'The Mixed Economy of A Democratic South Africa', p9.
12. Harris, 'Building the Mixed Economy', p8.
13. Quoted in *The Sunday Times*, 18/2/90.
14. The likely responses are summarised in Appendix 3.9

CHAPTER FIVE

MANAGING THE TRANSITION

Immediately after nationalisation, a government, faced with what to do with the enterprise, has three options. It can carry on running the company exactly as before. This means it becomes 'state capitalist' in its form and its day-to-day operations, with the state as the sole shareholder controlling the board of directors and deciding what happens to profits. The workers remain unionised and interact with the decision-making process as they do today — structurally outside of it, and negotiating through their unions. Their access to a share of profit is through annually negotiated wage increases. Other stakeholders — such as consumers — remain locked out of the production and marketing process. They can only vote in the market place by buying or not buying the product or service. This is what happened in Britain.

The second option is to get out and stay out. The government can simply redistribute the nationalised assets — through, for example, leasing — to worker, management-worker or consumer co-operatives. Alternatively the government could nationalise and install a new management which is directly accountable not to the government but to the workers, consumers and other interest groups, and responsive to the market. So long as the job gets done the government keeps its hands off the company. All decisions are made in relation to what is best for the firm and those interest groups pressurising the company's controllers. The government could, of course, step in at any moment since it has statutory ownership of the assets.

The third path is for the government to re-organise the enterprise along new lines. Among the many options there are: the social property mechanism as used in Peru — there it seemed to be a good idea but foundered for lack of economic efficiency and lack of support from the people who were supposed to implement it; the command economy concept of the Soviet Union, which also foundered for lack of efficiency and democratic participation from the very people who were supposed to benefit; the supported economy of Cuba, where nationalised companies had popular participation and support, but insufficient strength to survive without external assistance; or the production councils of Yugoslavia, where workers manage their own companies, participating in the profits produced.

When choosing an option the government should assume:

- Financial and operating efficiency is required;
- The aim is to generate a surplus where possible. If the nationalised company is a 'public interest' company which has to run, even at a loss, then the aim is to minimise loss;
- The nationalisation takes place under a government which aims to reverse the effects of racial discrimination;
- One aim of nationalisation is to achieve democratic participation, as far as possible, within the workplace;
- The takeover is not by way of confiscation;
- Effective control of the company rests in the hands of the state, management and the employees (or combinations of these) rather than outside shareholders.

The re-organisation option is the one being studied most closely in South Africa today. Indeed, it is the site of a key debate which could shape the future of nationalisation in South Africa: 'to own or to control'.

OWNERSHIP AND CONTROL

Government ownership or non-ownership as a means of attaining control over an enterprise is central to the nationalisation debate. There are two extreme positions:

- Ownership is the fundamental source of control. With 100% ownership the government is guaranteed control over the enterprise;
- Control is the most important target of nationalisation. It is not guaranteed at all by mere ownership.

This debate can best be illustrated by way of two examples — the nationalisation of the Zambian copper mines and the commandism of the Soviet Union.

The Zambian copper mines

In the mid-1960s the Zambian copper industry faced declining prices and was losing importance in the world minerals market. The copper mines, the third largest in the world, seemed to be near the end of their super-profitable life. All analysts predicted overproduction of copper by the 1970s as more producers came on stream — countries like Peru, Chile and Canada had increased their copper-producing capacity. The Zambian mineowners had to make a strategic decision: to expand, or continue output at current levels.

The government wanted rapid expansion since copper was its main source of foreign exchange and the most important contributor to GDP. Employment levels on the copper mines, stable for ten years, would fall if production did not increase. On the other hand, the two major copper companies, the Roan Selection Trust (RST) and Anglo American, did not want to increase their fixed investment in Zambia, particularly in the light of potential world overproduction. Also, the future of royalty and export tax arrangements was uncertain and the two giants feared the trend to nationalisation shown in other Third World copper producing countries.

As the Zambian government did not have the capital to 'go it alone' the capital expansions did not take place. But it then resolved the dilemma by nationalising the copper mines earlier than expected. The Zambian president, Kenneth Kaunda, announced the 51% nationalisation in his Matero Speech of 1969.

The joint venture Kaunda proposed was fatally flawed in that it depended on the companies providing control and expertise — without foreign involvement, and particularly that of Anglo American, the copper mines would simply not function. Since the *raison d'etre* of the nationalisation was short- and long-term expansion, the Zambians could not afford instability during the transition phase from foreign-controlled to government-controlled mining. The existing management, marketing and technological expertise had to be maintained, which was why a joint venture was proposed. These problems, combined with the timing of nationalisation — the price of copper was high at the time — enabled the negotiators of Anglo American to demand higher compensation payments. The Zambian government could offer favourable settlement terms of $180-million repayable at 6% over 12 years in foreign currency. It also proposed favourable future operating arrangements including administrative and technical services such as project consultancy, preparation of reports and financial statements, computers and management information systems and services, industrial relations, recruitment of expatriate staff, external purchasing services, provision of personnel, the preparation of business plans, viability studies, advising on production scheduling and the policy towards ore reserves and research and development. For these services a fee of 0,75% of gross sales proceeds plus 2% of profit after 51% mineral tax was offered. In addition there was an engineering service fee of 3% with all costs reimbursable. It was agreed that the Anglo American and RST companies would hold available funds for reinvestment in new ventures. Expansion of the mines was made a more favourable prospect by taxation changes. As a result of the nationalisation, majority ownership of the mines lay in the hands of the Zambian government. Control, however, did not.

> The difference between a 49% and a 51% shareholding did not mean the difference between a passive and an active role, for all practical purposes the ownership might as well have been 50/50. Mutual consensus and understanding would be a necessary prerequisite for a smooth operation and increasing development and no amount of legislation could provide an adequate substitute.[1]

The Zambian government did not end up with 51% of the profits either. The net economic benefit of the nationalisation for the Zambian treasury was nil. The annual recurrent effect on Zambia's foreign exchange position was 'between a loss of K15-million and a situation of no change, depending on the copper price' and 'the gain or loss as a result of such a major change as the mining nationalisation is remarkably small.' Increased cash flow to the mines was not utilised for capital expenditure, but to increased dividends and thus foreign exchange losses.[2]

The way the Zambian government structured the nationalisations gave nominal — but not real — control over the copper mines. That remained with Anglo American and RST. And the Zambians' objective of developing rapid expansion of the copper mines before the price collapse was not achieved, largely because operational and strategic decisions remained in the hands of the previous owners.

Soviet commandism

The Soviet enterprises were part of an economy driven from above by central planning. Producers were told what, when and how to produce. As long as they did that they faced no pressure to innovate or improve, or consider expanding facilities to meet other needs.

Wholesale prices, sourcing policy, wage levels, investment policy and the long-term existence of the enterprise were all controlled by an external administrative agency in the form of the central state.

The cost structure of the Soviet economy was determined by administrative and economic forces. The enterprise was required to cover operating costs, but usage of surplus and investment decisions were taken by a central administration.

This made it less responsive to consumer demand and technological changes because it had no real incentive to do so.

Commandism facilitated the administratively induced expansion of the productive base. But it proved far too cumbersome to increase productivity, improve product quality, or make use of available technology and raise the standard of living. It was unable to keep up with innovations worldwide because it was a closed and (supposedly) self-sufficient economy.

Ownership

Three questions arise: Should there be ownership by the state? If not, should there be controls? If ownership, how much and how controlled; and if control, through what and how much?

The Zambian and other experiences have resulted in an increasingly popular viewpoint that ownership does not matter very much — more important are the control of planning, competition and regulation. Such control, it is argued, can be achieved through government regulations and legislation, and without government ownership.

However, the track record of Soviet-style commandism has bred the view that too much ownership and too much control over productive activity is, in the end, counter-productive.

Murray argues that without the legal control and authority which ownership confers, implementing the aims of nationalisation is practically impossible. In the Greater London Enterprise Board (GLEB), for which Murray worked,

> trying to encourage the social aims of public ownership without equity control was like operating through a gauze. Private capitalists would, if necessary, agree to implement enterprise planning and equality programmes, but do all they could to frustrate their achievement.[3]

This is echoed among those in South Africa promoting the idea of black management, and of doing away with racist practices in firms — unless the companies are controlled by those solidly committed to these ideals, they will simply not find expression.

Structures of ownership and control are integral to the running of an enterprise, particularly if that enterprise is to become part of an overall co-ordinated economic strategy. But, ownership by itself is not the goal of nationalisation. Ownership does not necessarily confer control, as Zambia shows. Neither is it the case that state ownership — by mere virtue of not being private ownership — guarantees economic and social improvements in the economy or in individual enterprises.

Can such a balance between ownership and control exist? 'Socialisation' claims it can. This model advocates combining central planning of the macro-economy through a democratically controlled state, with democratic worker control at the micro-economic level.

Those who criticise Soviet commandism as an aberration of socialism now advocate socialisation as an alternative. In rejecting commandism they have also rejected nationalisation. Thus socialisation has come to be posed as an alternative to nationalisation.

The argument goes as follows. Private ownership vests extraordinary power and wealth in the hands of individual capitalists. Collective ownership is necessary to develop the basis for economic democracy, justice and equality. The only institution which can facilitate collective ownership is the state. Collective ownership through the state is a prerequisite for socialised production. But ownership does not guarantee socialisation and may result in commandism. So socialisation can only be achieved through placing control over the means of production in the hands of the producers.

But what is the difference between socialisation and nationalisation? Joe Slovo, general secretary of the South African Communist Party, wants to get away from old conceptions of nationalisation:

> The transfer of legal ownership of productive property from private capital to the state does not, on its own, create fully socialist relations of production, nor does it always significantly change the work-life of the producer. The power to control the producers' work-life and dispose of the products of labour are now in the hands of a 'committee' rather than a board of directors. And if the 'committee' separates itself from the producers by a bureaucratic wall without democratic accountability, its role is perceived no differently from that of the board of directors...
>
> State property itself has to be transformed into social property. This involves reorganising social life as a whole so that the producers, at least as a collective, have a real say not only in the production of social wealth but also in its disposal. In the words of Gorbachev, what is required is 'not only the formal but also real socialisation and the real turning of the working people into the masters of all socialised production.[4]

Davies too sees the Freedom Charter as a call for socialisation, not nationalisation: 'For a transfer of the monopolies to popular control to be complete it is necessary for the people to assume both the powers of economic ownership and the powers of possession.'[5] Powers of ownership determine investment, distribution of profits, and control over the accumulation process. The powers of possession relate to the organisation and direction of labour. The difference between nationalisation and socialisation is this:

> While nationalisation is a change in legal property relations, socialisation is a much broader process of collective reappropriation by producers of control over the means of production. Nationalisation...is a necessary element in a process of socialisation,.. (I)t needs to be accompanied, first, by the introduction of a process of planning in which social needs rather than profit increasingly becomes the criterion in decisions about the allocation of resources, and, second, by transformations in the organisation of management and labour processes which permit direct producers to assume increasing control.[6]

The socialisers want a completely different management style to plan responses to market forces. They want democratic collective management where decisions can be taken which will benefit the whole enterprise as well as the people in it. It is argued that the question of who controls the decisions distinguishes socialisation from any other system of production — be it state-managed nationalised industries or free enterprise systems. However, this is not the case. Capitalist management techniques, such as the Japanese quality circle concept, or participative management systems, make room for this form of decision making. There is little reason why nationalised state enterprises cannot be run this way either.

Socialisation also attempts to restructure the parameters within which market forces will operate — not by administrative fiat alone but by the state acting as a powerful agent within the economy. This agent should

> shift the balance of economic power from capital to the working class and the people... To ignore the question of democratic participation in the economy... is to tread a path which, from the point of view of social transformation, can only result in a *cul de sac*.[7] Furthermore, 'workers' participation at the point of production does not satisfy this desire for democratic participation.[8]

In this scenario the state would 'merely' own the enterprise. Socialisation would pass control of enterprises from private owners, not to the state, but to the direct producers in the enterprise. In this way, an enterprise would be 'socialised' (control passing to the direct producers) rather than nationalised (control passing to the state).

This conception can have two interpretations. Either it assumes that the owners of the enterprise (the state) would have no choice but to allow worker control, given that control is more important than ownership. This is a questionable assumption. Or it asserts that the state, once it has taken ownership of an enterprise (through nationalisation) will willingly cede control to workers. This latter view would not pit socialisation as an alternative to nationalisation. Rather, socialisation would be the organisational form nationalisation takes — in which case it is questionable whether socialisation is inherently different from nationalisation.

It is clearly different from the old Stalinist conceptions. But the Stalinist model is not the only one available. The distinction comes if one defines nationalisation merely as a transfer of legal ownership to the state. If this is the definition of nationalisation (which it usually is not, but came to be in the Soviet Union), then socialisation clearly is different to nationalisation. If a fuller definition of nationalisation is used, then the distinction becomes blurred.

What the advocates of socialisation are proposing is difficult to visualise precisely. They conceive of a form of nationalisation in which the state *owns* the means of production, but neither the state nor individuals nor committees *control* the means of production. Rather, the enterprise is 'socialised' and controlled by those who produce the wealth.

There is an unsatisfactory duality in the thinking: While control rests in the hands of the producers, ownership rests in the hands of the state. This could potentially result in dual power, where producers have day-to-day control and the state the ultimate say, with management caught in the middle. There would still be a tension between the need to trade off national priorities with enterprise goals. The state would not necessarily be willing to bow to producer control on such issues. Socialisation, while escaping the dangers of Stalinism and commandism, does not escape the dangers of state ownership in the manner the 'new socialists' would wish it.

The new socialists are looking for the determining partner in the relationship between enterprise and state. In reaction to commandism they assert that it should not be the central state. In reaction to capitalism, they argue, it should not be the managers of the enterprise. They resolve the question by saying: If the workers control the enterprise, and if the state is democratically controlled by the majority — the working class — then the state and the enterprise will be able to work in tandem, in complementary ways. The resolution of the problem is a question of democracy. The dualism remains.

And there is another problem: The commandism of capitalism has been criticised, where manager/owners dictate what happens in the company. But commandism from the central state is deemed unworkable. What the advocates of socialisation fail to recognise is that it is equally possible to have commandism by the direct producers — the workforce — who could run the enterprise in their own narrow interests, which are not necessarily identical to those of the rest of society.

The debate has advanced the critique of commandism and responded to the limitations of several past nationalisations, but socialisation has not necessarily provided alternative models for the future.

There is a resolution to the socialisation/nationalisation dilemma if one accepts that the state is the central judicial and economic agent for nationalisation; and that nationalisation by the state is the starting point for socialisation. Socialisation is not an alternative to nationalisation, but one of the forms it may take. It is a post-nationalisation process where the central issue is the relationship between the different stakeholders in the enterprise.

THE STAKEHOLDERS

Fundamental to successful nationalisation is the way the government takes account of the interests of the different stakeholders and their relative power. The stakeholders in the nationalisation process, and their key interests, can be:

- The government itself. It wants a share of company profits, or to minimise the losses it has to cover. It wants access to decision making, and for the company to be responsive to national planning priorities. These areas, in particular, are investment and financial policies of the enterprise, marketing, forward and backward integration and beneficiation policies, distribution of surplus, and overall objectives. It also wants the electorate to be satisfied with the performance of the nationalised industry and the economy as a whole.
- Workers in the enterprise. They want a share of the profits in the form of a living wage or better, access to decision making, decent working conditions (including health and safety, on-the-job training, advancement opportunities, welfare — paid leave, maternity benefits — and so on).
- Management of the enterprise. They, too, want a share of the income through a salary, plus benefits, or even a share of the profits; usually they want relative autonomy in decision making over control of personnel, production, sourcing of inputs, maintaining efficiency and the like; and opportunities for advancement.
- Consumers (individuals or companies) of the product or service the enterprise offers. They desire a quality product or service, cheaply. They require access to decision making about the service or product. This could be informal access through the market mechanism. If there is no choice of service or product, and the nationalised industry is a monopoly (or clearly dominant) then formal, direct access to decision making is required.
- Suppliers of inputs to the enterprise. They want the best price for their inputs, and a constant reliable market with clear criteria and requirements.

● Ex-owners. If the nationalised industry is paying compensation, they want certainty that they will be paid interest and capital amounts as promised.
● Society as a whole, through its interest in the impact of the nationalisation on state planning and the economy, redistribution and so on.

The structure of stakeholder involvement determines the form of the nationalised company and the guiding principles of company operation. The more their interests converge the more chance nationalisation has of working. This is particularly the case for workers, management and government, as Table 9 shows.

TABLE 9: The likelihood of success of nationalisation in relation to the convergence of interests of key players

Convergence of interests			
Government	**Workers**	**Management**	**Chance of success**
High	High	High	Excellent
High	High	Low	Fair
High	Low	High	Fair
High	Low	Low	None

As important as the convergence of interests — or lack of it — are the power relationships between the different groups. The more power a group possesses in relation to another, the more it is able to impose its will. Conversely, the less individual power the stakeholders have in relation to one another the less they are able to make nationalisation fail. However, if one group supports nationalisation and has a great deal of power in relation to other groups which do not support it, the more the pro-nationalisation group will be able to make nationalisation work. These relationships can be expressed in a matrix form.

TABLE 10: The four scenarios for nationalisation determined by the relationship between interests and power of different stakeholders

SCENARIOS FOR WORKABILITY OF THE NATIONALISATION PLAN

CONVERGENCE OF INTERESTS OF KEY STAKEHOLDERS		Low	High
	High	Certain success	Second best
	Low	Uncertain direction	The path to ruin

POWER OF KEY INDIVIDUAL STAKEHOLDERS (WORKERS, MANAGEMENT, GOVERNMENT) RELATIVE TO ONE ANOTHER

Where there is no identity of interests at all, and one stakeholder possesses far more power than the others and imposes its will, ruin is guaranteed. Each group will pull in a different direction, pursuing different goals. If the one group imposing its more powerful will is the government, then 'etatism' is the result. If workers exercise the greater power, there will be a continual dual-power dilemma, at least until the government is replaced. If the managers are dominant there will either be bureaucratic nationalisation, or no nationalisation at all.

Scenarios for South Africa

Where there is no identity of interests, and no stakeholder is dominant, the outcome is uncertain. Such a balance of power means one group will be able to frustrate the efforts of the others. For example, managers may simply not carry out government orders, or workers might refuse to implement management wishes. A clear outcome will be achieved by one of two means: either two of the key players form an alliance against the third and impose their will; or else there is a compromise or meeting of interests. This is the most likely resolution in South Africa should nationalisation occur — while there would be distinctions of interest between government, workers and management the first two groups are likely to ally against the third. How far along the power axis they can move is hard to say, since managers will possess a high degree of power by virtue of their concentrated skills.

If all key players are equally committed to nationalisation, and have an equal ability to contribute to its success, nationalisation is certain to work in South Africa. The best possible production systems, reward structures, redistribution mechanisms, innovation and so on could be designed. The government could contribute where required and the company could pull in the direction the state wishes it to.

If these key players fall into line with one another, it is likely other players will as well — or else be unable to stop the success of nationalisation. In the short term, given the disagreements about nationalisation, this scenario is unlikely.

In the second-best scenario in South Africa, key players have interests in nationalisation in common, but one group holds far more power than the others. This will lead to a situation where the efforts of nationalisation are seen to be the creation and preserve of that group; and potentially seen to be in the interests of that group. This will be harmful if it impacts upon democratic processes within the nationalised industry. While the industry would work to the benefit of all, it would not be driven by all. This is particularly the case if either the government or the managers are the dominant grouping. In the former case the initiative and control would appear to come from outside the enterprise, from politicians. In the latter case the managers are in a small minority, and would appear to be patronising in running the enterprise for the benefit of all. This situation could not last. Either there would be a jockeying for power by the other groups, or the power of the dominant group would manifest itself in the emergence of different interests. If there is a power struggle that leads to a more equitable distribution of power, and the identity of interests is maintained, then it is a recipe for certain success.

Between scenarios

From the above it can be seen that there is the possibility for movement between the different scenarios. The possible movements are shown in Table 11.

TABLE 11: Possible directions the nationalised industry may follow

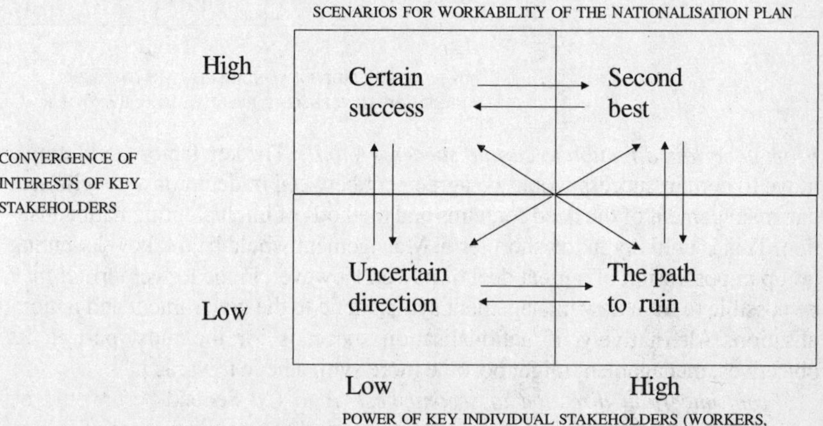

The matrix shows that many options are possible. One option could be as follows: assuming nationalisation in South Africa is characterised by a relative balance of power between government, managers and workers, all with differing aspirations, nationalised industries will start off in the Uncertain Direction quadrant. The possible movements from there are outlined in the Table 12.

TABLE 12: Possible directions for nationalised industry in South Africa

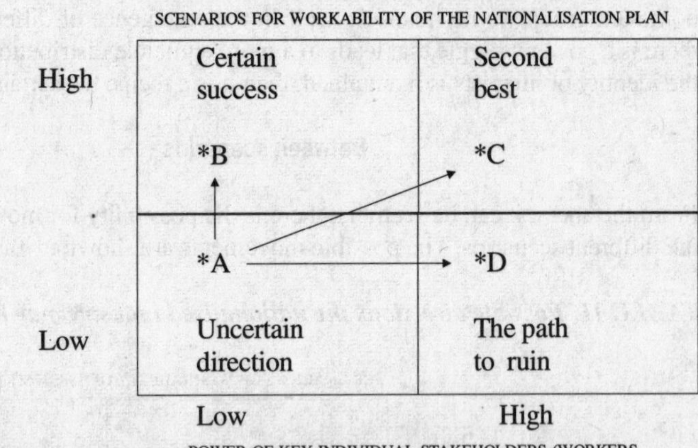

From uncertain direction to certain success (A to B): The key factor facilitating a move to certain success would be agreement between trade unions, government and management of the need for, aims and methods of implementing nationalisation. This is unlikely in the short term. Management would be the key dissenting group in possession of a great deal of power. However, in the longer term it may be possible to train new management sympathetic to the government and nationalisation. Alternatively, if nationalisation succeeds for the most part in its objectives, management might become more sympathetic towards it.

From uncertain direction to second best (A to C): Second-best would be achieved with a convergence of interests accompanied by a divergence of power. Given the fluidity of political power during processes of transition it is not altogether impossible that such power shifts could take place. However, for that to be accompanied by a convergence of interests is unlikely.

From uncertain direction to path to ruin (A to D): The key factor for such movement would be for one group to emerge as totally dominant and to impose its will on the other groups. Given the relative power bases of management, workers and government, it is likely that the emerging force would be either government or workers. If government emerges it is likely that this would be at the expense of democracy within political and enterprise structures. If workers emerge, a change of government which acts in the interests of the working class in an overt fashion is likely (the 'dictatorship of the proletariat'). It is probable that in the process the nationalised enterprise would cease to operate effectively, efficiently and democratically.

Seeking the optimum path

Clearly, in managing the process of nationalisation, a convergence of interests must be sought wherever possible. This is not easy to achieve for, at times, it appears that to give one group what it wants may have to be at the cost of another. For example, to achieve a low price for consumers might be at the cost of wages and salary for workers and managers, or at the cost of profits for the state.

Thus structures must be constructed in such a way as to manage stakeholders' interests. This will not be easy. Let us look at the example of the financial rewards demanded by each stakeholder, and assume the following (likely) conditions post-nationalisation:

- The government wishes to control inflation, and one leg of its strategy is to keep down prices;
- The government is spending heavily on social welfare programmes and needs maximum tax and other income;
- Workers in the nationalised company are unionised, and still struggling for a living wage;
- Management skills are in short supply;
- Management sympathetic to the aims of nationalisation are few, and most are motivated primarily by financial reward.

In this situation, all stakeholders have material financial interests they wish to realise:

- Consumers want a low price product or service;
- Workers want a living wage (or better);
- Managers want high salaries;
- The state wants high profits.

If the interests of the different groups are resolved by power alone, then the following will happen:

- Consumers are likely to be in the weakest bargaining position, particularly where they depend on an essential product or service for their daily existence, and even more so where the nationalised industry has a monopoly on supply. Consumer organisations are weak at present, and organising consumers nationally is a difficult process. Thus, other groups could achieve their material gains at the expense of price increases which consumers could not resist.
- The government is also in a weak position, since there are no guarantees for profitability. It depends entirely upon the efforts of management and workers to

run the industry. However, it can hire and fire, so it could replace those managers and workers not performing sufficiently well or not 'towing the line'. This is a potentially unwise exercise of nominal power as it might backfire in the long run. The government might have to live with being sėen as the 'boss' by workers, with workers and state in conflict.

- Managers, in the short term, can bargain strongly for a large slice of the financial pie. They have skills indispensable to running the company, which they can threaten to withdraw permanently. A manager's strike or departure could be sustained since managers can easily find jobs elsewhere. The company could well find alternative managers (depending on the skills shortage) and would probably be able to run the company relatively smoothly for a short period. But the effects of management action would be seriously felt on bottom line profits. They would thus be in a good bargaining position in times of skills shortages to bargain their salaries up.
- Workers, under nationalisation, would be immeasurably stronger than in a privately owned company if there were no government-imposed restrictions on the right to strike and organise. Their strong organisation, which probably led to the ability to nationalise the industry in the first place, would lead to their being able to win wage increases.

If the conditions outlined above hold, then it is likely the government would lose some income, consumers would lose out because of price increases, while workers and management benefit — not very different from what exists now. In other words, the struggle for material benefit from nationalisation by the different groups with a stake in the company would be the product of a power struggle over the spoils and the resources the company produces. Groups and individuals with most power would gain most relative to other groups. Some might say this is simply a continuation of the class struggle characterising South Africa at present.

If this continued class struggle, or racial struggle, is accepted as inevitable then nationalisation simply affects the terms on which it takes place and represents a swing in power away from capital towards the working class. The role the government plays would thus become a determining factor on the outcome of this struggle. If it comes down heavily on the side of the working class and consumers, management would end up with a smaller share of the wealth produced. Management, in this case, would most likely withdraw and seek better salaries elsewhere.

The government could come down heavily on management's side — either pragmatically wanting to retain management, or because the new bureaucracy's interest is obtaining a share of the wealth generated by the nationalised company. In this case it is likely that workers and consumers would conflict with the government. The government would face the potential of strike and lost votes.

It is possible that the government 'cops out', accepting that the wealth generated is divided between managers and workers in the form of higher pay packets for both. Either fewer resources would go to the treasury or there would be price increases for the consumers. Whichever the case there would be negative effects for the economy as a whole. The nationalising government will, immediately upon nationalisation, face certain questions mitigating against the 'cop out' option. As Adei points out:

> Nationalisation immediately puts some obligations on the state. These include ensuring adequate capitalisation of the firm; ensuring that people with the requisite know-how and skills are employed including an effective Board of Directors; and holding management accountable for firm-level performance. The state has now to perform the duties of sole shareholder.[9]

Adei argues that management accountability to politicians is possible, so long as the organisational structure and technological abilities within the enterprise are strong. Otherwise political intervention can wreak havoc. He bases this argument on the study of several nationalisations in Ghana. Mim Timber Company, with good structures and sound management, was well integrated into Ghanaian economic policies and strategies through 'political interventions' for this very reason. Other timber companies were hampered in developing sound operations by those very political interventions to which MTC responded so well. In fact, for those companies, the political interventions had 'disastrous consequences'.

> There is always a risk that nationalisation may lead to over-politicisation of vital decision-making processes within the firm. This price of nationalisation cannot be overlooked: the cause of the failure of nationalisation may be the politician.[10]

Thus, management of the stakeholders, and the relationship between them (or, if you will, the class struggle) becomes a central determinant of the probable success or failure of the nationalisation programme.

The question is: should the government regulate the relationship, given that it is itself a stakeholder, and given that the interests of its personnel might be in conflict with one or other stakeholders?

This is one of the arguments for the market mechanism. It does keep a check on the different stakeholder aspirations running away with themselves. Quite simply, the capacity for consumers to impose a very low price (through, say, the government) has a limit beyond which it is unprofitable to provide the product. For managers and workers to pay enormous salaries to themselves will impose high costs and consumers will simply not be able to afford the product or service.

The market mechanism is thus an essential tool required for managing the stakeholders. Its effects are felt immediately, posing an instant clamp on excess.

The government could decide to leave this short-term relationship between the stakeholders to the market, and rather manage the longer-term developments. For example, training new management would take many years. Eventually, however, it would impact by bringing more management skills onto the market, lowering the power of the management group. Since competent management would no longer be in short supply they could no longer make excessive demands. This, in turn, would free more financial resources for other stakeholders. Obviously, this would take decades to achieve.

The above example of stakeholder dynamics around financial reward has shown the centrality of managing the different stakeholders to the overall success of nationalisation. The experiences of Chile, Cuba, Peru, Zambia and many others have shown how governments waged war on the owners of industry — before they were in a position to win — and lost. In Venezuela the government attempted to take a 'consensus' approach, moving all stakeholders slowly in the same direction. Opinions differ as to their success.

The position taken by the government on this question will fundamentally shape the form the industry takes post-nationalisation.

NOTES

1. Faber, MLO and Potter, JG, *Towards Economic Independence: Papers on the Nationalisation of the Copper Industry in Zambia*, Cambridge University Press, Cambridge, 1971, p102.
2. Faber and Potter *Towards Economic Independence*, pp123-125.
3. Murray, R, 'Ownership, Control and the Market' in *New Left Review*, July/August 1987, p103.
4. Slovo, J, 'Has Socialism Failed?', *South African Labour Bulletin*, (14)6, 1990, pp17-18.
5. Davies, R, 'Nationalisation, Socialisation and the Freedom Charter' in *South African Labour Bulletin*, (12)2, 1987, p92.
6. Davies 'Nationalisation, Socialisation and the Freedom Charter', p94.
7. Wolpe, H, 'Democracy and Economic Planning in the Mixed Economy: Some Preliminary Comments on Recent Papers', paper prepared for the ANC-Cosatu Conference on the Post-Apartheid Economy, Harare, April 1990, p3.
8. Wolpe 'Democracy and Economic Planning in the Mixed Economy', pp3-4.
9. Adei, S, *Technology Transfer and Nationalisation in Ghana*, Industrial Development Research Center, Canada, 1987, p106.
10. Adei *Technology Transfer and Nationalisation in Ghana*, p107.

CHAPTER SIX

OWNERSHIP AND ACCOUNTABILITY

A new government in the process of nationalising industries has many options when structuring ownership. One is, of course, full state ownership, or 100% nationalisation, which can be structured in a number of different ways:

- As departmental agencies with the same legal personality as the government, staffed by civil servants and financed from the government budget. Examples might include health, education and some welfare institutions.
- As public corporations with a separate legal personality, usually created by a law which defines the corporation's powers and duties. Their financing is often through loans or allotments of capital and not by the issue of shares. Obligations to the state would include implementation of policy objectives, including production and expenditure obligations, and limitations on resource usage and the sale of assets. Examples which already exist in South Africa include posts and telecommunications and nuclear installations.
- As state companies established under ordinary company law, controlled by government through its ownership of the majority of shares. Examples have included utility companies (electricity, water) and transport companies. In these cases, the assets are owned by the state, and companies operate on full cost accounting procedures and compete with the private sector.

Under these latter two arrangements the state could either manage the enterprise entirely itself or enter into a management contract with private capital.

Partnerships

A different option in the nationalisation process involves partial nationalisation. Various forms of partnership agreements include:

- Over 51% ownership, as in the case of the Zambian copper mines;
- Minority ownership of ordinary shares (less than 50%);
- Minority ownership of special shares (such as 'golden shares') which vest powers of majority ownership in the state .

Where the state takes a majority or special shareholding, it can leave managerial control in the hands of the private minority shareholders. The state could also enter into partnerships with other shareholders, which can include the following scenarios:

- The state retains possession of natural resources but leases them out to private companies for exploitation;
- State enterprise enters into agreement with private firms (often multinationals) for a joint venture;
- The state enters into joint-venture agreements in strategic industries;
- The state nationalises 100%, and then sells a part of its shareholding to selected partners (private or co-operative).

There could even be tripartite state-worker-private sector partnerships.

The joint venture form offers a reduction in risk of expropriation, or it may be a 'way station' to full control. Where there are constraints — such as access to capital, skills and technology — it could be advisable for the government to enter into joint venture agreements.

> (A joint venture) maintains access to...marketing, managerial and technological expertise — and avoids the traumas of nationalisation, while simultaneously assuring the government of ultimate control of decisions affecting the national economy.[1]

Joint ventures can lead to conflict between the government and its private partner, making management control a key issue. Areas of difference and agreement could be specified in advance. If there is agreement on efficiency and profitability within the firm, management could be given the role of overseeing that, subject to policy approval by the government. It is in the areas of investment policy, hiring and firing, marketing and the like that disagreements are likely to occur — with government aiming for specific objectives in this sphere.

Some argue that it would be wiser for the state to enter these partnership agreements with worker-controlled enterprises as these are less likely to see the obligations involved as an interference with ownership rights to the extent that a capitalist would.

Options for such a partnership are Employee Share Ownership Participation Schemes and Profit-Related Pay (PRP). Esops have, in the South African context, become something of a swear-word to unionists and workers. In the present South African political-economy 'they have been shown' according to one author, 'to offer no improvement in economic performance in the absence of worker participation in management and they make no impact on redistributing economic power and wealth.'[2] The same author believes that Esops and PRP aim at

> weakening trade union organisation and militancy, they offer no shift of management control to the workforce, they are often introduced to pass the costs onto employees of rescuing or restructuring the company or plant, and there seems to be no systematic relation between such schemes and economic performance *unless* worker participation in management is incorporated.[3]

Given the hardening of this attitude among unions and workers, it is unlikely that Esops or PRP systems on their own will be accepted after nationalisation. However, if they are accompanied by some form of real power within the enterprise, attitudes may change.

Most often, nationalising governments use a combination of different ownership forms, the range of possibilities limited only by the imagination of the planners, and the workability of the forms. The example of Peru illustrates this.

Joint ventures and mixed ownership in Peru

The Peruvian military government of the 1960s aimed to create a mixed economy which was neither capitalist nor socialist. Three means were used to achieve this:

- Developing a state sector through nationalisation. These state companies would continue to run as they had before, and the workers experienced them as if they were capitalist enterprises.
- The second means involved the establishment of Esops, which in Peru were called Industrial Communities, which required up to 50% of shares in profits and ownership to be distributed to workers. Foreign investors were to sell out a percentage of their holdings, on a fixed schedule, to local investors.
- The third means developed in 1974 when the Velasco government announced the Social Property Law authorizing the establishment of worker-owned and worker-managed enterprises. This law was the product of consultations with a

diverse range of local opinion, as well as with foreign advisors from the US and Yugoslavia. The aim was to gradually establish Social Property Enterprises.

> (SPEs would be) run by a general manager and board of directors, elected by an assembly made up of all the workers in the enterprise. Each year, in addition to wages, the workers would receive a share in the 'surplus' (profit) of the firm proportional to the number of days they had worked.[4]

The law also provided for the allocation of funds for housing, health and other worker benefits. This fund would be run by a board partly appointed by the government and partly elected by the participating SPEs. The firms would pay the fund back for loans advanced. They would then carry on paying a 'capital rental' to fund the expansion of the Social Property sector. The firms could also raise capital through issuing 'stockbonds', the income from which would be tax exempt.

Establishing SPEs proved difficult. There were problems developing equality between the firms since some were rich and others very poor. There were also problems in the relationship between this sector and the private sector because of the tax advantages enjoyed by SPEs.

Despite imposing a special tax on company profits (10%) to finance SPE formation, the main stumbling block to the growth of SPEs was the lack of state funds. After two years there were three SPEs in full operation, 48 in formation and 500 still under study.

SPEs were not formed out of the nationalised companies. The SPEs were mostly small, and involved either the initiation of new enterprises or the acquisition of an inefficient or bankrupt private firm. The government tried to discourage worker takeovers 'from below' by requiring a two-thirds vote of owners, partners and shareholders, as well as bureaucratic processes, before the firm could be approved for SPE status.

The SPE programme never reached fruition. There was extensive opposition from investors, the International Monetary Fund and foreign governments. Local capitalists were unhappy with the situation. Then in 1975, after runaway inflation, massive indebtedness and the drying up of investment capital, the military government was overthrown in a bloodless coup. The change in government signaled a reversal of previous policies.

The new president, Morales, privatised large parts of nationalised industries. Interestingly, a committee appointed to evaluate the SPEs found that they worked — and would be retained — only in labour-intensive enterprises which were financially self-sufficient. By 1977 only six SPEs were in full operation and 34 'in formation'. The Industrial Community scheme did not apply to enterprises with 25 or less employees, and worker share ownership was cut to 33% for the rest.

One reason advanced for the failure of the Industrial Community, Social Property and nationalisation programmes was the method by which it was done — it was imposed from above. Those who gained from the policy were not the rural poor or the urban unemployed. 'The real beneficiaries of the Velasco reforms were the upper to middle sectors (still in the top 25% of the income distribution pattern of Peru), including urban bureaucrats, members of agrarian co-operatives, and, especially, unionized workers.'[5] This is not dissimilar to the profile of those who might benefit from the same programme in South Africa. In addition, the reforms were expensive:

> If there is a lesson to be learned from the Peruvian experience, it is that in order to carry out internal reforms without a violent revolution a government must be in a strong economic position... Without such a position, attempts to control or take over foreign corporations are seriously limited by the continuing need for foreign technology, markets, and above all, foreign financing.[6]

Producer co-operatives

If the state chooses to nationalise and then 'get out' there are several ways in which this can be done. Setting up producer co-operatives with collective ownership structures is one. The entire share capital could be transferred either directly to individual workers in the enterprise; or to a trust which operates in the interest of the producers, controlled by producers (with or without state representation). The obligation of the co-operative to the state would be in the form of tax.

Producer co-operatives are different from capitalist and state enterprises in that they are both owned and managed by members who are also its workers. This option is favoured by those who believe that producer co-ops are democratic, non-exploitative and yet efficient methods of production. Others disagree:

> One advantage that is claimed for co-operatives is that they do not operate on the basis of exploitation, but in fact they often do. Their members are often directly exploited by other enterprises, for modern production systems mean that co-operatives often work as subcontractors where all aspects of their production and the price they are paid are controlled by the large corporation to which they are contracted. And members also have an incentive to exploit other workers for, if they hire non-members, the members' profits are increased by following capitalist practices.[7]

Very often, co-ops are subject to such strong competitive pressures that they have to operate in the same profit maximising way as small private firms and adopt the same management techniques even though they are owned by their members.

In theory co-operative production may appear to be democratic and non-exploitive. But the practice is different as co-ops operate in a competitive environment, interacting with the market. Protecting the co-operative from the rigours of the market mechanism must mean that the producer co-operative is not an efficient structure to control production.

> Producer co-operatives do not provide a third way, and they do not avoid the necessity for formulating and evaluating specific policies for state enterprises and private enterprises.[8]

There are many who may take issue with Harris. Gorbachev's planners in the Soviet Union are looking at different forms of producer co-operatives to regenerate economic growth through encouraging limited individual equity, and incentive.

Consumer co-operatives

There are two main types of consumer co-ops:

- Non-profit organisations;
- Consumer-owned companies.

In the United States and Britain, non-profit organisations have emerged as viable enterprises. These companies are primarily service industries, or production companies for direct sale to customers with high level of involvement. They include, for example, companies which build houses for electricity and other utility companies. All these non-profit enterprises are funded by a combination of state and private funds. In some all shares are owned by users.

They are run by a board, which sets wage levels, plans corporate strategy and so on. Some have a direct relationship to the government — mainly through funding — and have at least one director from the government (be it central or local government). The closer the company is to the customer (the more decentralised the control is) the better these structures work.

No individuals 'own' the non-profit company, and none are allowed to appropriate the surplus generated in the course of providing the service. Given the 'consumer control' of the company, the surplus that is generated is returned to the consumer — both directly and indirectly.

Take, for example, an electricity consumer co-operative which generates a profit which it wants to return to the consumer. The consumer would be paid a cash amount which is deducted from electricity bills each year. This could affect an amount paid some 15 years earlier, putting refunds on a 15-year cycle, which is an indirect funding of the business. Alternatively, the funds could be put back into the business, into improving the service, into research and development and into new plant and machinery.

Obviously, direct consumer control is limited to such enterprises where consumers have a daily relationship with the company, and can get to understand its dynamics. It would not work for a company which marketed manufactured goods such as toilet soap or televisions.

It may be possible for this form of ownership and control to find expression in South Africa. For instance, after the boycott of electricity in Soweto, Eskom proposed either to sell the electricity utility company to the local authority (the Soweto Council) or to privatise. Community representatives rejected this proposal and demanded a form of ownership whereby neither the state nor individuals would own the electricity supply to Soweto. Rather, the people of Soweto would either own shares, or the supply company would be bought out by a non-profit organisation controlled by the residents of Soweto. It would be a not-for-profit company controlled by the consumers.

This may be the ultimate form of 'market-driven' company, and would get around the question of responding to the market. In terms of service industry management, this would be the ultimate form of 'customer involvement'.

Lease-back and franchise

After the economic failures in Eastern Europe and the severe economic challenges in the Soviet Union, economists turned to lease-back arrangements to regenerate the economy. Under lease-back the state retains ownership of the assets, but relinquishes control. An individual, co-operative, joint venture or other body could, for a fee, lease the asset for a lengthy and fixed period. During that period that body can do what it wishes with the asset within limits agreed to before-hand with the state. The fee could be fixed by a variety of formulae — for example, a fixed amount to be paid at regular intervals, or an irregular amount linked to profitability.

Lease-back is thus still part of a state-owned sector, but not a state-managed sector, and it could be argued that it is a form of privatisation.

Leaseholding may be an alternative to the land distribution question in South Africa. The state owns the land and issues leaseholds to different forms of production. Dolny suggests that individuals who are victims of forced removal should have their land reinstated via marketable and hereditary leasehold; land taken over by the state should be made available for rental or purchase by individuals, a collective or a community; collectives should also have leases which are marketable; and joint ventures should buy land on leasehold or sell land it does not wish to farm. Erwin suggests that:

> the most effective means of the state gaining control over land and natural resource usage would be for the state to constitutionally own such assets. This would open the way to more complex ownership structures since such a constitutional step need not be followed by the state exercising its right of ownership immediately.[9]

It could do this by forming large land trusts, to be used for small farmers and co-ops, backed by state-run training and resource centers. In areas such as mineral exploitation it could effect its policy objectives through lease-back arrangements (which could even embody compensation) to existing owners. This proposal is not very different to what exists at present. Under South African law, the government owns all minerals and sells the mining rights to private companies.

Franchising could be structured to work in the same way — particularly in service industries. Under franchise arrangements the state would retain control of corporate planning and finance, but would franchise out the provision of the service or the running of the utility to private or co-operative ventures.

STRUCTURING ACCOUNTABILITY AND CONTROL

Much of the attention of those proposing nationalisation in South Africa is taken with two main questions: how the nationalised industries are to be efficient and generate funds crucial to an ailing economy; and how the public — and workers — are supposed to benefit and be heard. Designing the institutions of accountability has become a key concern.

Accountability is fundamental to the operation of public enterprise, and needs to be far more than the financial accountability which characterises the private sector.

> (Public enterprises) cannot be left with the same degree of independence and secrecy of decision making as companies in full private ownership — indeed, if they were, there would be little point in taking them away from such ownership. It follows that the commercial type of audit... cannot suffice (though it may have a role to play)... Political and public opinion demands more.[10]

However, the question which has plagued governments, economists, managers, workers and the public is: how much accountability? One answer reveals just how troublesome the solution can be: 'more accountability than that of private companies but less than that of ministerial departments.'[11] Trite as that may seem it provides a valuable guide which should be borne in mind: state enterprises are not private industries, but nor are they government departments. They need different structures of accountability and control. There are two polar positions on the accountability and control question, with a range of answers in-between:

- The ultra-autocratic: the enterprise should be accountable to its management. If management performs badly it would be fired by the shareholder — in this case the government.
- The ultra-democratic: the enterprise should be accountable to all who have an interest in it — including workers, consumers, the government — indeed, the public at large.

Structures of accountability for the first position are easily set up — a management board consisting of government representatives to whom the managers report. In the second case the structures are complex — too complex, say some, to be workable.

Most experiences of control and accountability fall somewhere between those two extremes. For example, traditionally socialists argue for accountability to the workers in the enterprise (rather than to management) and to the government. However, most often the consumers, suppliers and the general public are left out of the equation, the assumption being that the government will properly represent them.

In 1920 the British Labour Party proposed a sophisticated monitoring apparatus to ensure accountability and efficiency of nationalised enterprises. The machinery aimed to ensure a free flow of information through a tripartite representative board of management, employees and consumers overseeing daily issues; and a standing parliamentary committee as well as independent monitoring bodies, voluntary associations, consumers and others looking at matters of policy. On daily issues the board was to be autonomous, although monitored. On policy it would be subject to parliament. This public information would be fundamental to establishing democratic control including:

- Consumer councils, which would support consumer interests;
- Parliament (in a variety of guises);
- Both financial and efficiency audits, some undertaken by semi-judicial bodies;
- An outside body to which, for example, price increases would have to be justified. This would generate publicity.

This position was influential in the British Labour Party until nationalisation actually happened under Morrison post-1945. He favoured unfettered specialist management, with labour and consumers left to influence policy from outside through unions and consumer councils. Management was charged with acting in the public interest (which was left undefined). Government ministers would also keep an eye on managers of the boards to ensure they acted in the public interest. Thus, in the British nationalisations, owner-management and professional management of industry motivated by profit was replaced by specialist management motivated by public interest. But it remained unclear how public interest was supposed to be heard, or whether it was a replacement for the profit motive. In leaving the definition of public interest to the government minister of the day, the door was opened to excessive 'politicisation' of the nationalised industry, a politicisation which fluctuated as the governments changed.

With these factors in mind, structuring the company should take account of the primary relationships it wishes to establish — to the government, the consumers, and others, as well as the accountability it must have to the market.

Company structures are a function primarily of the relationships to external and internal forces. These forces could be composed either of groups of people (shareholders, workers), institutions (the government, the laws), the environment or economic forces (supply and demand, competition, the market, inflation).

Once again there are two extreme positions — which parallel those of the ultra-democratic and the ultra-autocratic:

- The enterprise should respond primarily to market forces;
- The enterprise should respond primarily to the needs of those working within the company.

The way the company wishes to relate to external forces and arrange internal forces will determine its structure. This relationship is captured in matrix form in Table 13 and 14:

TABLE 13: The impact of external and internal forces in determining the company structure

INTERNAL FORCES		EXTERNAL FORCES: Weak	EXTERNAL FORCES: Strong
	Strong	Inward looking	Balance
	Weak	Uncertain	Outward looking

TABLE 14: The logic driving the company

RESPONSE TO EMPLOYEE DEMANDS		Low (RESPONSE TO MARKET DEMANDS)	High (RESPONSE TO MARKET DEMANDS)
	High	'Welfare organisation'	Dynamic antagonism
	Low	Directionless	Ruthless efficiency

The dynamic captured in Table 14 is not a simple process — it involves competing priorities and contradictory demands as captured in the relationship of 'dynamic antagonism'. The company can find itself caught between two antagonistic logics: 'the market, which requires straight competitiveness, and public service, which requires a great deal of philanthropy by company standards.'[12]

The antagonism becomes evident when each logic is separated out between different organisational forms — if the company responds to the market and the government responds to public interest. 'One can expect the company to defend its own interests in the name of competition and to fight government instructions based upon a broader conception of public interest.'[13]

The dynamic is further complicated when one considers that control and accountability can be to groups outside of *or* internal to the enterprise.

Accountability to a board

In an attempt to simplify these dynamics, a government could stay out of any structures of accountability, exclude workers or consumers from the echelons of power, and simply retain an expert management. Many British nationalised industries were run this way, and have been heavily criticised for this.

In the United States, the nationalised Tennessee Valley Authority (TVA) was put under the control of such a management board.[14] The TVA is a nationalised company owned entirely by the American government. The heart of its operations involves control over the water and natural resources of the Tennessee River drainage basin and its adjoining territory in Tennessee and seven other states. The area covered is almost the size of Britain. Based on this it has interests in hydro-electrical power generation, fertiliser production, river navigation, civil engineering works, fisheries, flood control, retarding soil erosion, afforestation, land and industry planning, improvement of agriculture, proper utilisation of marginal lands and conservation and utilisation of the basin's other natural resources. By the mid-1970s it operated on a budget of $4-billion annually.

The TVA is not bound simply by the generation of efficient electricity, but is also committed to develop the geographic region. It aimed to develop the standard of living for the people of the Tennessee Valley region and to enhance the existing quality of life through economic development and community services. To this end the TVA developed other services for poorer communities. By 1970, the Community Development Program provided garbage disposal and assistance to 100 communities; it trained firemen and adapted surplus army vehicles as fire appliances; provided dental services in parts of North Carolina and Georgia, regional co-operative libraries in Alabama and survival rooms for the old; did solar-energy research; controlled nuclear waste; promoted wildlife conservation; provided health centers, and much more.

The TVA was championed by Republican senator GW Norriss in 1924 when he proposed the nationalisation of railroads, shipping, nitrate plants and electricity generation in the Tennessee Valley. Eventually, in 1933, president FD Roosevelt nationalised diverse enterprises and established the TVA, saying it 'should be charged with the broadest duty of planning for proper use, conservation and development of the natural resources of the Tennessee River drainage basin and its adjoining territory for the general social and economic welfare of the nation...'[15]

The TVA is a large and effective utility corporation run on competitive capitalist lines. It competes directly with privately-owned companies, mainly in the power industry. From the start the privately-held companies attacked the existence of the TVA, increasing in hostility as the TVA became more successful in producing cheap electricity.

The TVA fixes the rate it charges to cover all costs, including interest on its borrowings, and leaves a small margin (an approximate 5% surplus). It is one of the cheapest sources of energy in North America. Innovations in fertiliser production based upon the availability of cheap electricity led to the sale of fertiliser throughout the United States, and the adoption of its methods by other companies. Welsh believes, from his study of the TVA, that:

> The fact of public ownership confers great opportunities. Governments can direct nationalised industries to the public good; they can be a test-bed for enlightened research and development, both in their own technical sphere and in human resources. They need not be bound by that concern for consistently increasing short-term profits that is a major bane of a market-financed company.[16]

The TVA Act set up an unusual form of control — what Welsh calls a 'democratic dictatorship in the form of a triumvirate'. Each member of the board was to have tenure for nine years, but at different times. The US president appoints successors. The board had extensive powers — to hire and fire, set salaries, define duties and design the organisation. The first board members were an agronomist, an engineer and a lawyer. General managers were appointed from the ranks of TVA staff.

Besides having a wide scope of reference the board was accountable directly to the president, not to any government department. This means that the board is, in effect, not accountable to the government but to itself. Despite these extensive powers, the board's guiding philosophy was essentially democratic. Said the second general manager in 1938:

> Democracy is the efficient translation of majority desire into public benefits; the success in doing that is dependent on quality of personnel and good working relations. We have no worship for organisational charts...but we need an organisational arrangement. The personnel craves some definition of its duties so that it can learn with whom they must co-operate. You cannot have budget control unless you fix responsibilities, and you cannot cut red tape or simplify procedures where there is administrative confusion. There are many approaches to organisation. From one viewpoint an organisation is a democratic institution consisting perhaps of little social units. From that viewpoint you want freedom of speech, the mechanics of committees perhaps, majority rule, an educational approach, and the modern ingredient of collective bargaining.[17]

Such democracy in planning was, for example, used to design the community and the houses for workers servicing the development of a large dam in the Valley. For customers, the TVA develops plans with smaller communities in the poorer regions to improve industrial facilities.

Whilst the TVA is run from above by the board and the general manager, it has attempted to draw in the public. This is partly a political move designed to develop strong public support which could resist the pressures that emerge from time to time from private business, congress and the senate to privatise or change the terms of reference of the TVA. One of the presidents to whom the board was accountable, Eisenhower, referred to the TVA as a 'communistic organisation'.

More importantly, however, public accountability is the method by which the TVA maintains its support-base. The difference between the TVA's public accountability and that of political parties is that the TVA board cannot be dismissed. If it was not fully open and accountable it would be easy to label the TVA as an undemocratic dictatorship, but it avoids the label as information on all aspects of TVA work is publicly available:

- Annual reports are comprehensive, cheap to purchase and available to any member of the public;
- The board is subject to congressional hearings when it seeks to increase its permitted borrowing limits, which must be sanctioned by congress. Government departments can submit reports and questions on the TVA, as can unions, consumers and others.
- The TVA holds public board meetings every two weeks, either in its headquarters, but also covering most of the main centers it services. These meetings are open to anyone, agendas are handed out, television and press are present.

Such meetings cover everything from explaining new innovations in power generation to answering questions from consumers about electricity rates, presenting the accounts for a quarter, and running through borrowing policies.

The consumers of TVA electricity are themselves organised into pressure groups and given access to the board meetings. One such group is the TV Industrial Committee, representing 32 industries, which itself commissions firms of accountants to analyse TVA finances and operations. Unions also attend the meetings. Welsh concludes that:

> the overwhelming case for open board meetings of the TVA type is that only in this way can institutions be made directly and consistently aware of the feelings of consumers, suppliers, workers and the public and, conversely, be given the opportunity to explain their policies, and to be seen to be willing to modify these in the light of public debate.[18]

Despite optimism about the structure of accountability, many consumers in the area complain of a lack of accountability. Said a representative of the consumers' East Tennessee Energy Group:

> The voice of citizens is too frequently ignored in the TVA's decision making process. The so-called public meetings...or rate reviews are merely comment periods on decisions already taken, and thus because they are so meaningless they are poorly attended.[19]

Without public support and participation for such forums, however well intentioned the board is, the company will not be fully accountable to the consumers and others. However, its operations include valuable ideas which could be incorporated into broader structures of accountability, and which attempt to get around the over-politicisation of the company. And there are alternatives to handing over control to professional managers and well-intentioned directors.

One way of combating the 'politicising' trend of the government is to have other, equally-powerful, sources of influence involved in the decision-making process. These sources could be the financial world and the trade unions. Each step of the corporate strategy could be planned with these groups, spelling out the financial and labour implications at each stage. Long-term contracts could be agreed upon by customers. If there was a national plan from central government into which the industry had to fit — and which might entail unprofitable service or product provision — the costs could be calculated into the strategic plan or even charged to the national plan in the form of subsidies.

However, one must be careful not to treat trade unions as an adjunct to the process, laying down their interests in deference to the needs of the corporation: 'Where new skills were needed, training programmes would be provided; where redundancies were necessary unions would be warned...'[20]

Taking the approach that diverse sources of power would balance one another, the principle developed for consumer representation could be extended to include other groups besides consumers. A board could be set up with representatives from government, labour, environmentalists, consumers, financiers, suppliers, management, scientists, retailers, distributors, and even others with a material interest in the company. While accountability to these groups might be necessary and correct, it is at this point that accountability and control must be separated. Should the state enterprise be controlled by such diverse groups, it is unlikely that any decisions would ever be taken.

Accountability to government

Accountability of the nationalised enterprise can be to parliaments, courts, ministries, special bodies, courts of auditing, and many other structures. The structures of government can influence nationalised industries directly, by taking decisions (for example on prices, investment decisions, deficit financing). There could also be indirect influence *ex ante* by appointing the enterprise's board, or *ex post* by financial and managerial auditing or by criticisms or inquiry and by adjudicating disputes (for example between the enterprise and consumers). The major types of control the government can impose upon the enterprise are:[21]

- Bureaucratic control, which exists in America through the General Accounting Office (GAO), in France through the Court of Accounts (Cour de Comptes) and in Italy through the Corte de Conti. Strangely enough Britain's state enterprises do not fall under the control of the Exchequer and Audit Department (EAD), although there are other bureaucratic structures controlling their operations.

Bureaucratic controls tend to be more formal than real types of control, and have not worked primarily because they are unsuited to entrepreneurial activity or a constantly changing environment requiring diverse and innovative responses.

● There can also be control by direction, where the government lays down guidelines and targets for the enterprise. The major problem has been working out which agency provides the direction. Most often (as in Britain and France) there are several government agencies involved, which leads to fragmentation of control.

To work, this form of control must balance autonomous day-to-day controls with longer-term imposed controls. In Italy there has been extensive debate about the legitimacy of laying down guidelines for public industries, but not for private industries. When guidelines were laid down for all, they ended up being ignored, except by state industries.

● Financial control is probably the most effective form of control a government has over a nationalised industry. Through controlling the funds allocated to the public enterprise, the treasury or relevant ministry can insist on certain levels of performance, on set levels of efficiency and so on.

This control depends upon the financial weakness of the enterprise. The better an enterprise is doing the less financial control there will be.

● Control through information. Through demanding full information (particularly on finances, operations and planning) and disclosing it to the public, the government can control the enterprise. To be effective, this approach requires extensive information research and preparation, as well as management willingness to disclose information. It also depends on the level of accountability demanded by the public.

● Market-oriented control is a newer form being attempted in countries ranging from Italy to the Soviet Union. This includes contracts between state and public enterprises introducing competition among different enterprises.

● Efficiency control. An 'efficiency audit' replaces financial control to ensure the efficiency of the enterprise, that there is no exploitation of a monopoly position if it exists, sound industrial relations, correct quality of product, in the correct quantities at the correct price; and so on.

● Full Cost Accounting (FCA) is a means of introducing economic incentives to correct the problems of commandism. The government sets the parameters within which market forces and economic incentives emerge, and then minimises its administrative intervention. 'Full cost accounting provides economic incentives that generate a responsiveness and efficiency in a corporation that is healthy. Public ownership combined with this form of accountability can best achieve broader social objectives.'[22]

Etatism

The most extreme form of central government control is etatism, where all aspects of civil and economic society are controlled by the central state. The Soviet Union under Stalin was a prime example of this, while the command economy is the economic expression of etatism.

Under etatism the nationalised enterprise is tightly controlled by one person appointed by, and operating under the orders of, central government. The central government is characterised by many layers of bureaucracy. Production schedules, pricing, marketing, pay scales, even quantities produced and bonuses are determined by this bureaucracy which uses mathematical models to cope with the vast problems of planning and controlling nationalised enterprises.

Since all planning occurs at a central level, there is little drive for quality, cost control, innovations and efficiencies at the level of the firm. All that matters is reaching the targets set at the centre. The device for managerial and operational control is the fulfillment of the production plan. A good manager meets the plan; a bad manager does not.

Over-centralisation means there is no response at all to market mechanisms. There is no competition between firms and there is no method of judging whether the enterprise is producing what the market needs. This is for two reasons — there is a lack of information flow (since it flows to the centre as information and comes back to the enterprise as commands) and the market mechanism is distorted through central control over consumption patterns. Since the consumer has no choice but to buy what the central state delivers, there is no return information to the enterprise. The only indication of consumer need is queuing, which indicates quantity problems.

Thus, while central planning does make possible the speedy mobilisation and rapid re-allocation of resources, commandism under etatist government gives no autonomy at all to the firm. Control is tight and centralised.

Control through parliament

In Britain, there are different structures of accountability to parliament:

- Various committees, including some specifically for nationalised industries, but also those for accounts and treasury;
- Debates on annual reports submitted by the nationalised industry which are tabled in parliament by the relevant minister;

● Parliamentary questions, submitted in writing to the relevant minister. Often these questions are not answered, particularly if the questions relate to the day-to-day activities of the enterprise;
● Financial debates on Bills setting up, or altering, the terms of borrowing powers, wage increase formulas and the like.

Despite all these forums, parliamentarians have found it difficult to develop real accountability of the nationalised industry to parliament. Parliament is now seen in Britain (as in France and Italy) as having limitations when it comes to controlling the nationalised industry;
● Reports from nationalised industries are usually long and complicated, and inaccessible to the average member of parliament;
● Time limitations mean the parliamentary forum can never consider the strategic plans, financial structures and so on in any depth;
● The industry becomes a political football for the official opposition and the government to kick around. The opposition would always want to prove the nationalised industry was not working under that government, while that government would always be convinced it was doing no wrong.

In his review of 30 years of the relationship between nationalised industries and parliament, Kelf-Cohen concluded:

> Parliament has been forced to look on, with a feeling of helpless indignation, at the fact that it has but little part to play in supervising this development (of nationalised industries). 'Parliamentary accountability' has proved a will-o'-the-wisp.[23]

Furthermore, there are a whole series of relations with government outside of parliament which are important as well: to the treasury, government departments, and sometimes review boards and the courts. It is difficult for members of parliament to keep track of, or influence, these relationships.

Control by a minister

Where it has been difficult for the average British parliamentarian to hold nationalised industries accountable, it has been easier for the minister in power to do so — if s/he is so inclined. Ministers in Britain were given the power to define policy and issue general economic guidelines:
● Ministers could appoint or dismiss chairpersons and members of boards;
●The minister was empowered to issue general directions to the board — for example the application of surplus revenue; had to be consulted on corporate plans; and could set financial targets.

● Boards required ministerial approval when reorganisation or expansion needed substantial capital outlay on capital account as well as in relation to training, research and education. Ministerial consent was needed for borrowing.

Under this system British nationalised industries have found it almost impossible to maintain a consistent, long-term strategy. Throughout the 1970s nationalised industries were under government pressure until in 1981, prime minister Thatcher forced most of them to abandon their expansion plans. After several major strikes were crushed, the Conservative government either suspended capital expansion plans or privatised outright.

It has been a consistent criticism that successive British governments have interfered in long-term planning by treating the nationalised industry as another mechanism for instituting party political policy. This is one of the greatest dangers that arise from putting politicians in charge of industry.

The holding company

A holding company is widely used to form a single umbrella structure for several (sometimes several hundred) companies. This can be geared toward a controlling function or for ease of management, controlling prices, achieving co-ordination between different entities, and so on. Examples of this are ENI and IRI in Italy, the Zambia Industrial and Minerals Corporation, INA in Spain, Renault in France, NDC in Tanzania and many others.

A holding company can be helpful in translating public-control goals into meaningful directives to management, far more expertly than government departments can. It can serve as a sounding board, complete with data, for government social and economic policy on public enterprises. A holding company can also set up and monitor control mechanisms, measures of efficiency, and performance indicators appropriate to each set of subsidiaries, rather than use a single set of blanket targets. These can be linked to indicators of social performance.

A disadvantage of the holding company is that it does not overcome the tension between accountability to its subsidiaries and accountability to the government. The more it is accountable to its subsidiaries the less responsive it will be to the public interest. The reverse is also true. Achieving a balance will be a challenging task. Furthermore, given that the board of a holding company can be very powerful, there is a potential to set up a conflict between the holding board and the sectoral ministry or minister in charge. There could be conflict if there is a power balance or if the ministry attempts to control the operations, effectively replacing the function of the board.

Holding companies tend to attract ministers or senior politicians to their boards (the president of Zimco is Kaunda himself). This defeats the purpose of separating government from management. If the holding company covers diverse sectors its competence to take decisions requiring expertise will be limited. If it concentrates on a single sector this would not hold. Possibly an investment advisory council for nationalised industries could oversee, or review, plans for financing industries. Experienced businessmen and bankers could be found for the council.

Conflicts between government and nationalised industry

One of the main reasons for opposing the involvement of government in structures of control over enterprise is that there is 'inevitably' conflict between those who run the company and those who run the government.

What determines the level of conflict between government and the enterprise? Based on seven case studies of major conflicts between government and state enterprise in France, the following conclusions were drawn by Anastassopoulos:

- The nature of the industry is irrelevant — the level of technology, capital or labour intensity, maturity of the product market, or the degree of instability of the sector does not determine the situations or level of conflict;
- State-owned enterprises feel threatened when they believe their strength as separate entities is threatened;
- The degree of interaction between government and company is important — when there is a large degree of company autonomy from the government there is likely to be more violent and overt conflict;
- Government challenge to strong national or corporate plans — if there is a strong corporate plan, widely accepted and adopted within the company, there will be resistance to government interventions. Either management or unions could enter into conflict over this with the government. The same is true if government has a clear national strategy which it feels is not being supported, or is being negatively impacted, by the state enterprise;
- The degree of market competition faced by the state enterprise is irrelevant;
- The success of the company is not as strong a factor. Rather, the conflicts always concerned decisions which would have a direct and strong impact on the company's performance or its survival.

Accountability to consumers

In profit-driven industries there is a high degree of responsiveness to consumer attitudes (otherwise known as part of the 'market mechanism'). Competition theoretically alows the consumer choice, and in that process propels the companies towards being more efficient and effective in providing what consumers want. The company that is most effective obtains more profit as its reward.

With nationalised monopoly industry, on the other hand, there is little incentive — neither for profit nor from competition — to provide an efficient and effective service. In some cases — like electricity and water — consumers have no choice but to use the service provided. There is no impact on the managerment of other sorts of nationalised industries as consumer withdrawal of custom does not bankrupt the enterprise as it would a private firm.

Thus, accountability to the consumer must be strengthened and consumer-driven efficiencies and effectiveness institutionalised. This is most easily done through consumer councils. It is debatable whether the consumer councils could either replace — or be as effective as — the processes of market forces in all industries. Some industries would lend themselves more to consumer councils than others. It is interesting to look at the 'independence-public accountability dilemma' from the point of view of the consumer.

> On the one horn efficiency seems to require the large-scale organisation which almost inevitably means a measure of monopoly. The other horn is that a corporation which is unchecked by competition can keep the gains of efficiency — if there are any — for the people who work in the industry instead of passing them on to the consumer. So the public body which grants the monopoly bows to the need for public accountability by establishing controls to make sure the monopoly does not abuse its power. The problem...has been to achieve this surely laudable objective without so hampering the corporation by fussy government intervention that the efficiency sought is not in practice achieved. A monopoly can be a giant; but shackles can shrink him into a pygmy.[24]

When coal was nationalised in Britain, Harold Macmillan protested that those who controlled the monopoly fixed prices for the industry. In reply the Labour government set wages by profit levels, which in turn were set by price levels. Ministers as a result were reluctant to fix prices (and consequently wages) themselves, beyond using the general price control powers already available to the government. Instead they used consumer councils, or consultative councils, to set prices. In effect the councils were face-saving instruments for the companies and the minister. Thus was the idea of consumer councils born in 1946.

In 1956 a parliamentary select committee looked at ways of strengthening these councils. It recommended that the councils:

- Should be actively promoting consumers' interests instead of being an impartial channel for two-way communication between producer and consumer;

- Be consulted by the industry about future plans, and major policy changes;
- Be given effective means of representation on issues of prices;
- Be financed by the ministry rather than the industry to give them independence;
- Be allowed to do expert research;
- Have representation at all levels — from local to national — and develop committees at all levels.[25]

It was recommended, however, that managements should remain independent of the councils, leaving councils in an advisory and representative capacity only.

But consumer councils' input is usually complaints-based. They may thus not provide for communication *between* company and consumers or company communication *to* consumers, but only *from* consumers.

The conclusions and recommendations of the commission were as follows:

- Consumer councils should exist. They should be housed together, and should develop a research facility with a large body of knowledge;
- The councils must give protection to the consumers in two ways: where individual consumers have failed to get satisfaction from the industries; and by pressing the interests of consumers about prices and standards of service. The councils should 'set targets for their industries — consumer objectives as standards against which the performance of nationalised industries could be properly measured... Agreement between consumers and industry on performance objectives would in the nationalised industries be a substitute for the yardstick of customer satisfaction by which private industry should be judged;'[26]
- The commission considered the recommendation that nationalised industries should not be able to raise prices or reduce service without the approval of consumer councils. However, it rejected this on the basis that this would give too much power to the consumer councils. 'If the councils controlled prices they would in effect be the boards of the industries.'[27] Rather, the councils should be informed when there was to be a price change and be given a chance to make representations on behalf of the consumers;
- Councils should be represented on the boards of the nationalised companies involved, when the independence and consumer commitment of the councils was not in question. This would help advance consumer interests during initiation of industrial policy, rather than after the fact by ensuring debate of consumer issues at the highest level; by giving the council early warning of the coming changes; by ensuring access to operational and financial information; and by giving the consumer authority within the industry;
- Both industrial and commercial users should be on the councils along with domestic consumers. This would add expertise.

Extending these principles, consumer councils could operate on all levels — national, regional and local — almost in a mirror image to the way a company functions. Ideally, the company should incorporate these structures, but would be unlikely to carry out the functions sufficiently well given the agendas of both management and labour.

Consumer councils could cater for the interests of different consumers. For example, in electricity there are industrial and household consumers. Household consumers include housewives as well as the elderly — thus, given the diversity of consumers, maximum participation could be gained from specifying the market segments, and giving them representation on the council. This would prevent domination by the largest interest group, and possibly overcome the 'shareholder apathy' so prevalent in South Africa.

In the United States some government-owned companies operate as if they are consumer co-operatives. While ownership rests in the hands of the government, control rests in the hands of users, or customers. The consumer of the electricity or housing scheme participates at the annual general meeting of the company. The users elect the board and set down guidelines by which it functions. In one electricity company in the US, there are 35 000 users, and all these consumers are invited to the board meeting. They have equal votes, irrespective of the amount of electricity they consume. A small customer is thus as important as a big customer.

Accountability to workers

There is a substantial body of opinion in South Africa which argues that all industries should be under 'worker control'. Usually this means the control of those directly employed in the industry (rather than any broader definition of the working class) represented through their unions.

The assumption underlying this position is that if nationalised industries work in the interests of workers, then they will work in the interests of the society as a whole. This is not necessarily the case — as much as it is not the case that if the nationalised enterprise works in the interests of the government then it will work in the interests of society. The function of trade unions is to represent their members' interests — as workers at the point of production. It is questionable whether everything workers demand through the union will be in the interests of the enterprise, or the consumers, or the government. For example, an improvement in working conditions, while being necessary in many places, is a costly undertaking. It is a cost that must be borne by the consumers or the government. At some point improvements in working conditions need to be weighed up against other needs. Trade-offs will be required, which workers may not be in the best position to make, unless they are to act outside of their self-interest. Outright worker control thus needs qualification.

Alternative approaches call for 'participative management' and 'industrial democracy'. But these are broad terms open to differing interpretations. It could mean joint decision making, consultation of workers by management, workers' control, or passing some functions of management on to workers.

Management and workers will probably take differing positions on these issues. Management is unlikely to consider workers skilled enough to take decisions on issues crucial to the enterprise. Workers are unlikely to trust management sufficiently to give them autonomy. The resolution of this dilemma is not easy. There are several possible approaches:

- Structural solutions, incorporating workers into the decision-making process at all levels. Participative management could be designed structurally, to incorporate representation at all levels, or functionally, where applicable. It could be the task of the management committee to co-ordinate and balance these processes;
- Corporate planning can be internally generated, with worker and management participation. The plans could then be taken to other stakeholders, including shareholders (if any), financiers, customers and suppliers, and government;
- Train worker representatives in the skills of management.

While the development of democratic participation in decisions and planning might unleash a potential and productivity previously unrealised in South African industry, there may be a flip side to the coin. Participative management may cause problems for management. Managers, particularly in South Africa, are used to solving things themselves. Now they will be required to meet with worker representatives and discuss solutions to problems. Worker representatives, on the other hand, might well feel that nationalisation will have been a victory for them. Where once managers had complete autonomy in decision making they now have to consult workers. If not well handled, this could become a difficult situation.

In this context it may be that both management quality and style changes. Decisions at lower levels might attain significance that, prior to nationalisation, they might not have had. Small issues once easily solved might be turned into large issues of principle. Decision-taking might thus turn into decision-passing as smaller and smaller issues are referred upwards for 'final consideration'.

Worker directors

Several nationalised industries in Britain adopted worker-director schemes as the means for developing worker participation in management. Some of these schemes (like British Steel) were later dropped. Most did not work.

In a study conducted into worker-director schemes it was found that:

- Worker-directors were expected to participate on boards with the same style and agendas as other board members. The role of worker directors was seen to be the same as that of other directors — they were simply expected to be ordinary directors and were not supposed to generate broader participation;
- Worker-directors wore two hats — one as participants in the board's decisions (to which representatives would have contributed) — and one as union representatives. These two roles inevitably conflicted, dividing the worker-directors' loyalties. The only alternative was to become exceptionally bureaucratic and refer all decisions back to the union for consideration. This would cripple the enterprise's decision-making ability and response time to problems. In any case, it was found that the level of contact between worker-directors and the union dropped the longer workers occupied their new posts;
- The worker-director was usually inexperienced relative to other board members. S/he depended almost entirely on other board members for information and inevitably ended up adopting the viewpoint of the board on most issues;
- This was exacerbated by the degree of management hostility. Either this was sophisticated and the interaction characterised by attempts to 'co-opt' the worker-director, or it was outwardly hostile, making the development of trust and a working relationship — key to participative management — impossible;
- There were often several places where policy development took place — ranging from management board to directors' meetings to executive boards to planning committees to sub-committees. If workers are only appointed to management boards they have no access to these other key policy-making areas. Other directors could thus limit the extent of worker participation in planning and policy formulation. As a result it was found that the effect of worker-directors on policy formulation and management style was limited. There was not so much worker-participation as a single worker participating on the board.[28]

Other structures

There can, of course, be combinations of the different forms of control outlined above. These include:

- Structures of dual control (management-worker, or worker-state);
- Tri-partite control (management-worker-state);
- Broad coalitions (tri-partite plus other interested groups and/or specialists).

One group which must be singled out for consideration is the provider of capital. This could include banks and shareholders (where there is a joint venture or partnership). Accountability to this group would not necessarily be through personal representation of the providers of capital. Accountability could work through the discipline market forces would bring to bear on company operations, and the company's obligation to meet interest payments on the debt or dividend payment on the equity.

Banks might go further. Often their provision of loans is made dependent on the submission of a strategic plan which the bank considers acceptable and workable. This plan would have specific targets set out for growth over a certain period, for a target capital structure, and for management of key ratios. Should the targets not be met, the loan could be recalled. Efficiency would be imposed at arm's length, through the market mechanism.

CONCLUSIONS ON RESTRUCTURING

South African mining, manufacturing and farming sectors are characterised by white ownership and management, employing cheap black labour which, for the most part, has little information on the businesses it works for, let alone any say in running the company. Management style is paternalistic and sometimes tyrannical, with labour — broadly speaking — being treated as a factor of production which can be brought in (hired) and moved out (retrenched) almost at will.

Outside the context of nationalisation, these structures of ownership and control, and the management methods to which they give rise, need restructuring. Those advocating nationalisation have stated this as one of their aims. Nationalisation would be an instant beginning to this process. As a result it would receive enthusiastic support from those excluded from management and ownership at present. By the same token, managers and owners are most likely to resist, feeling (correctly) that management prerogative is being intruded upon.

The restructuring of ownership and control would therefore be the key interface in the changing power relations between capital and labour. Labour would wish for an acquiescent management, content to work for less-than-exorbitant salaries, and willing to share strategic and operational decisions with worker representatives. Labour's organisational muscle and influence over the government would be used to achieve this end.

Management, to the extent that it is prepared to work in nationalised industry, would want a free hand to interpret market signals and make the necessary adjustments within the enterprise (particularly by hiring or firing at will). Its justification would be that management expertise facilitated dispassionate judgements, unconfused by party political interests, in the best interest of the company and its shareholders. Control over skills and information would be used as the bargaining chip to win arguments.

The problem confronting a future government, if it undertakes nationalisation, is complex: how to restructure ownership, establish an appropriate relationship between the state and the industry, democratise nationalised industry, restructure management control systems, while retaini_ skilled, top-quality management. There are three approaches to restructuring:

- Business as usual: This is not an option — there would be a contradiction between the form of ownership and the form of control. The government would immediately set itself up in an antagonistic relationship with unions, one of its main support bases for nationalisation in the first place. This would also contradict all policies which aim to redistribute wealth and power on a non-racial basis;
- Get out and stay out: While this is more of an option it is also unlikely. If nationalised companies have been targetted using the 'strategic' method proposed above, they would be key to the economy's growth and long-term well being. Transferring ownership of such assets to worker, worker-management, or consumer co-operatives would be unwise. Beside going against some of the original motivations for such key nationalisation, it is unlikely that such co-operatives would be able to marshal the skills and resources required to manage such enterprises. However, the state could transfer ownership, or lease other assets. For example, some categories of land could be transferred to farmers; producer co-operatives could be encouraged in assets of less strategic importance. Some argue that the state should do this wherever possible;
- Re-organise along new lines: This is the most likely option, and certainly the one which would be applied in the 'strategic' commanding heights nationalisations. This does not imply only wholly state-based forms of ownership. Mixed forms of ownership could include partial state ownership, partnerships, mixed ownership, Esops, and golden share schemes (whether worker or state).

Ownership is one of the major vehicles by which the state is able to influence the running of the company — despite arguments that ownership is not key.

However, restructuring cannot be left there. This is a point made with emphasis by the proponents of socialisation. Ownership without control is useless. Control without participation is commandist.

Managing the transition in South Africa

In any process of transition, the dynamics are delicate. It is particularly important, in transition from private to nationalised enterprises, that ownership and accountability structures used take into account the different interests, and functions, of the stakeholders. The path restructuring takes is a function of inherited structure, and the demands of the external and internal environments.

A newly nationalised company inherits an old structure representing a different set of relationships and priorities. If it is to transform this, it must manage the process very carefully. Structural design should balance external and internal factors which make business work, as well as human and commercial interests. People inside and outside the enterprise must be integrated into serving the specific market of the business in such as way as to give the enterprise competitive advantage. Unless this balancing of commercial and human interests is achieved, the enterprise will not achieve the goals of nationalisation.

A range of workable options of ownership and control forms present themselves for use in the South African context. There are no easy options, or options guaranteed to achieve their ends.

Given the current ANC, SACP and Cosatu criticisms of commandism in the Soviet Union under Stalin, it is unlikely that a future South African government will opt for commandist forms of ownership and organisation. It is also unlikely that nationalisation will resemble the process in Great Britain: there is a stronger commitment from pro-nationalisation ranks in South Africa to democratic structures than was shown by the Labour Party; the context of nationalisation and the time in which it would take place is very different; and the lessons emanating from the British experience have been learned.

Accommodating different interests

The restructuring process should seek to incorporate different interest groups involved in the company. A key interest group is 'the government', an all-encompassing term for economic planners, ministers, the treasury, and representatives in parliament. Since representatives of this particularly large and diverse interest group plan the nationalisation and carry it out, they are usually responsible for designing the structures of accountability which follow. It is not surprising, therefore, that maximum accountability is generally to this interest group — others coming a distant second. It is also not surprising that accountability has usually taken a governmental-bureaucratic form, whether in Britain or the Soviet Union.

Other interest groups include the consumers, whether companies or individuals — for whose benefit this is all being done but who are seldom brought into the process — workers and management of the enterprise, and the providers of capital, whether they be the government, banks or the equity market.

The question is often posed as to which is the 'most important' interest group. The answer then determines how accountability should be structured. If the workers are most important, then they should have most of the say; if management is the key to success then its control over the decision-making processes should go unchallenged; if the government, as the new owner, is fundamental then it must be able to direct the enterprise.

But a key to the success of nationalisation depends, at the outset, on workers being accorded far more power to participate in key decision-making processes than they have at present, and management and government accepting that this should be the case. Success also depends on workers' acceptance that management's function is specialised, and that responsibility and authority must be delegated to management to carry out that function. Success depends further on management and workers accepting that the government has a role to play in the enterprise insofar as it fits into a national plan to build a strong and competitive economy. Finally, the success of nationalisation depends also on workers, management and government accepting that consumers should be able to state their interests, both indirectly through the market mechanism where it is efficient, and directly through representatives.

Dangers to consider, mistakes to avoid

As the case studies above have shown, there are potential dangers involved in restructuring:

- Developing accountability to and control by a single group (government, workers, management or consumers) which runs the company in its exclusive interests;
- Allowing too much 'involuntary' control, for example through market forces;
- Trying to control 'too much', and allowing too little possibility for market forces to influence the enterprise;
- Putting sole control into the hands of groups (particularly government, consumers, workers) who lack the expertise to run the enterprise;
- Confusing the powers of possession (ownership) with the powers of control.

Mistakes have clearly been made in the nationalisation process which resulted from not restructuring ownership and/or control correctly. Proponents of nationalisation can learn from these mistakes. But there is nothing inherent in nationalisation which made these mistakes inevitable. Nationalisation does not imply a set of immutable organisational forms. In fact, it opens up entire new possibilities. While there are dangers and pitfalls, there are also workable options.

An increase in democratic participation in the structures of control and accountability does not by definition preclude increased efficiency and workability. Indeed, this may be a precondition for its long-term success. Control can be decentralised to good effect.

There are controls imposed by the market which are irreplaceable in developing efficiency and effectiveness. These should not be removed, but rather enhanced where possible, and their negative effects mitigated in other ways. It is possible, too, for other structures of accountability to impact unintentionally upon the operation of the market forces. Thus an environment needs to be structured in which the signals coming from the market can be easily seen and interpreted. Doing away with market forces may make it easier to manage the different stakeholders, but more difficult to manage the enterprise.

Structures of accountability and control

Options for the structures through which interest groups can interact with the firm include:

- A holding company, which facilitates the participation of management and the government, but can be set up to incorporate other interests;
- Investment advisory councils, which bring in experts from the private sector or universities;
- Golden shares, which give government or workers the controlling vote in all decisions;
- Consumer councils;
- Production councils with worker directors, balancing management and worker representation; and
- The board structure, which can be flexible enough to include representatives from government, workers, management, consumers and others.

These can all operate at centralised or decentralised levels, with decentralisation being geographical or functional. The structures which offer the most potential for participation, accountability and control are combinations of:

- The board structure, which includes government, management and worker representation;
- Decentralised decision-making within the enterprise. There should be broad consultation about corporate strategy, and productivity and performance targets within the enterprise;
- Consumer councils, particularly where state enterprises are monopolies, should be instituted. These, too, should be decentralised as far as possible.

Building accountability and designing forms of control has previously been seen as the responsibility of agents external to the enterprise. The problem with control-via-Act-of-Parliament is that it is *imposed* accountability, with external agents trying to keep control, act as watchdogs, and ensure performance. This is often perceived as being detrimental within the enterprise.

It would be far more effective if the push for accountability came from *within* the enterprise. This would lead to management and workers finding forms of accountability which would build the enterprise as well as make it accountable. At the very least those agents within the enterprise should be able to promote forms of accountability best suited to the enterprise's mission. Examples around the world show that when a bureaucracy is the focus of the control and accountability mechanism, the system does not work. But financial controls are effective and should be maintained, but should focus more on controlling efficiency.

Promoting good management of the critical success factors, in addition to meeting financial and other performance targets is of central importance. The enterprise should be run efficiently internally, and effectively in relation to the needs of the consumers of the product or service. Improvements in quality of product and correct pricing techniques should be a focus.

Prior to the computerisation of industry, the capacity to use information as a form of management control was limited. However, as information systems have developed so has the ability to monitor and control business. Where management information systems have been used as a tool for internal accountability, they can be adapted to serve the accountability process more generally. Full information disclosure in an accessible form should facilitate accountability. Developing this capacity must be a priority in any restructuring process.

The institutional forms of socialisation

Table 15 summarises the different forms of ownership, the likelihood of their use in South Africa, and the possible forms of control to which they might be subject:

TABLE 15: Possible forms of ownership and control envisaged for nationalised industry in South Africa

Ownership form	Likely in SA	Options for control structure
Wholly state-owned	Yes	Governmental;consumer council; board with worker, management, state representation; market.
Partly state owned	Yes	Golden Shares; governmental; board with management, owner, state representation, maybe worker and consumer reps also; trade unions.
Joint ventures - State-worker State-private	Yes Not very	Governmental; board with state, management and worker reps, consumer council, trade unions
Producer co-ops	Yes	Producer, market control
Lease back	Yes	Producer, market control

From the above table it is possible to extract the different forms of ownership and control envisaged by the advocates of socialisation. Slovo has said that socialisation, in practical terms, means developing

> worker participation at enterprise level... I don't mean that an economic project can be governed by a show of hands day-to-day... (But) producers...and consumers...must be involved beyond the market in seeing how things are produced.
>
> The state (would) control the enterprise in co-operation with trade unions, insisting on a style of management which gives workers certain participatory rights — not necessarily profit rights — consistent with the need to have hierarchies of management and decision making processes... I am talking about something that would give real power to workers, even if ownership remains partly or majorly in existing hands....[29]

To this can be added other elements of socialisation: full cost accounting and lease-back (particularly of land) to producer co-operatives. From this we can derive the organisational model described in the following table:

TABLE 16: The organisational model of ownership and control envisaged under socialisation

Forms of ownership envisaged	Forms of control envisaged
Wholly state owned	Government control, consumer councils, producer councils, trade unions, participative management, dual control, market control.
Partly state owned	Golden shares, dual control, tri-partite control, consumer councils, participatory management, trade unions, market control.
Joint ventures (state and private capital)	Dual or tri-partite control, consumer councils, unions, participatory management, market and government control
Lease-back to producer co-ops	Producer control, market control
Private ownership	Participatory management, producer control, consumer councils, trade unions.

It is revealing what is *not* included in this model by the 'new socialists':

- Forms of ownership not mentioned at all include state-worker partnerships, Esops, consumer co-operatives, franchising, tri-partite (management-worker-state) ventures;
- Although mentioned, producer co-operatives are not emphasised;
- Parliament and ministerial control are not specifically mentioned, although this could be implied by 'governmental control';

In addition there is antipathy to undemocratic management, even where there is private ownership; etatist forms of control, bureaucratic controls, and excessive and unilateral intervention by government. The 'new socialists' demonstrate a strong commitment to diverse forms of ownership, democratic forms of control and the strong assertion of market forces. This bodes well for finding workable organisational structures, and avoiding some of the mistakes of the past. But there are no guarantees.

Accountability to the market

By far the biggest and most unresolved debate involves the relationship between state enterprise and the market. Market controls are being advocated in the Soviet Union, Great Britain, Italy and elsewhere, as well as in South Africa. But they can take different forms:

- Some argue that monopolies, whether private or state, should be forbidden. State enterprises should rather be broken up into competing sub-enterprises. A whole sector of industry should never be nationalised. If this happens, competition is killed. Only a part of an industrial sector should face nationalisation. While this is a logical position to take, it should not be made into a religion. Some monopolies do work. And there are often good reasons why monopolies develop insofar as they are products of the market forces (for example, there are significant savings on economies of scale, or there are experience curve benefits). Deciding when monopolies should and should not be allowed is, however, a thorny issue and yardsticks are not easy to develop;
- Priority setting should not be too 'politicised' but should respond more to market messages than to government. Government could determine the constraints within which the market should operate, but once it has done that it should stay away from functional decisions. If it intervenes to correct decisions taken by the state enterprise which it sees as wrong, this is because the constraints set by the state are not working correctly. Impeding the ability of the state enterprise to manouevre within those constraints will ultimately harm its efficiency;
- Where possible the enterprise should be forced to face the possibility of bankruptcy — the ultimate market mechanism — by not having its existence guaranteed by state funding. This would particularly be the case if the state nationalises a well-functioning, profitable industry.

If market forces are the key pressure to which a company responds, it is difficult to ensure that it will act in the public interest. On the other hand, if the government provides the key pressure then it is difficult to ensure that the company will act in its own commercial interest. The trick for public enterprise lies in finding a mid-way which will accommodate the best interests of the individual company and at the same time act in the best interests of the public.

NOTES

1. Sigmund, P, *Multinationals in Latin America: The Politics of Nationalisation*, University of Wisconsin Press, Wisconsin, 1980, p292.
2. Anonymous, 'Populism Without Robin Hood?: Forms of Ownership and Control in a Post-Apartheid South Africa', paper prepared for the ANC-Cosatu Conference on the Post-Apartheid Economy, Harare, April 1990, p3.
3. Anonymous, 'Populism Without Robin Hood?', p14.
4. Sigmund, *Multinationals in Latin America: The Politics of Nationalisation*, p208.
5. Sigmund, *Multinationals in Latin America: The Politics of Nationalisation*, p220.
6. Sigmund, *Multinationals in Latin America: The Politics of Nationalisation*, p220.
7. Harris, L, 'Building the Mixed Economy', paper prepared for the ANC-Cosatu Conference on the Post-Apartheid Economy, Harare, April 1990, p7.
8. Harris, 'Building the Mixed Economy', p7.
9. Erwin, A, 'An Economic Policy Framework', unpublished draft paper, 1990, p30.
10. Normanton, EL, 'Accountability and Audit' in Vernon, R, and Aharoni, Y, *State-Owned Enterprise in the Western Economies*, Croom Helm, London, 1981, p167.
11. Normanton, 'Accountability and Audit', p168.
12. Anastassopoulos, JP, 'The French Experience: Conflicts With Government' in Vernon, R, and Aharoni, Y, *State-Owned Enterprise in the Western Economies*, p99.
13. Anastassopoulos, 'The French Experience: Conflicts With Government', p99.
14. Information on the TVA is drawn from Welsh, F, *The Profit of The State: Nationalised Industries and Public Enterprises*, Maurice Temple Smith, 1982, London.
15. Quoted in Welsh, *The Profit of The State*, p95.
16. Welsh, *The Profit of The State*, p112.
17. Quoted in Welsh, *The Profit of The State*, p99.
18. Welsh, *The Profit of The State*, p123.
19. Quoted in Welsh, *The Profit of The State*, p128.
20. Welsh, *The Profit of The State*, p189.
21. Cassese, S, 'Public Control and Corporate Efficiency', in Vernon, R, and Aharoni, Y, *State-Owned Enterprise in the Western Economies*.
22. Erwin, 'An Economic Policy Framework', pp31-32.
23. Kelf-Cohen, *British Nationalisation, 1945-1973*, Macmillan, London, p133.
24. National Consumer Council, Great Britain, Parliament, 1976, 'Report Number 1: Consumers and the Nationalised Industries', prepared for the Secretary of State for Prices and Consumer Protection, London, 1976, p2.
25. National Consumer Council, Great Britain, 'Consumers and the Nationalised Industries', p11.
26. National Consumer Council, Great Britain, ' Consumers and the Nationalised Industries', p80.
27. National Consumer Council, Great Britain, ' Consumers and the Nationalised Industries', p81.
28. Prosser, T, *Nationalised Industries and Public Control: Legal, Constitutional and Political Issues*, Basil Blackwell, Oxford, 1986, p135-150.
29. See interview with Joe Slovo in Appendix 1.

CHAPTER SEVEN

WEIGHING THE RISKS

Those who question the very idea of nationalisation in South Africa have not lacked arguments. Chiefly, they have drawn attention to the following:

- Nationalisation has not worked elsewhere;
- Nationalised enterprises are not motivated by profit and end up being a drain on government coffers;
- Nationalised enterprises are not disciplined by market forces and competition;
- Politicians are risk-averse and therefore make bad owners;
- Decision making in nationalised enterprises becomes politicised;
- Management may be badly motivated and inefficient.

Critics of nationalisation point to nationalised enterprises around the world to show that it has not worked — steel and coal in Britain, the re-privatisation of banks in France, copper in Zambia. They also point to failed economies — many in Africa, some in Latin America and, of course, Eastern Europe and the Soviet Union. These economic failures, they say, are the result of nationalisation.

But enough examples of successful nationalisation can be found to undermine the argument that, as a rule, nationalisation does not work. The point remains, however, that many nationalisations have failed. This reality cannot be swept under the carpet and the lessons of those failures should be learned.

As part of the state, nationalised industries have access to a bottomless pit of funds. There is no threat of bankruptcy, the ultimate market discipline, which gives little incentive to profit. Unprofitable, the enterprise ends up being a drain on the exchequer. When the enterprise looks elsewhere for funds it will be difficult to find lenders, and there will be little retained profit. Bond payments (if applicable) will most likely end up not being honoured.

Socialists claim that they have never been against profit *per se*, and have always advocated the need to generate surplus. Their complaint has always been with the manner in which profit is produced, and the way it is distributed under capitalism.

The lessons of Eastern Europe and the Soviet Union have in fact pushed the supporters and critics of nationalisation closer together in agreeing on the importance of the profit motive. Slovo thinks the profit motive 'most important'. Generating a surplus, he says, 'must be a key aim of all enterprises except in those areas where, for social reasons, the state goes in for complete subsidisation.'[1]

If there is agreement, in principle, on the importance of the profit motive the question remains how this motive will remain without the threat of bankruptcy.

Market forces and competition

One of the most prevalent anti-nationalisation arguments is that nationalised firms do not have to operate within market forces, or in competition with other companies. The assumption is that the government usually nationalises a whole sector rather than a single company.

Competition is key to maintaining efficiency and becoming effective in the market, particularly where the nationalised industry produces a consumer product. The drive to increase quality and decrease costs is lost without competition.

Without the market mechanism, pricing structures will be distorted, resulting in under- and over-production. If market forces do operate, political interference in decision making will prevent the nationalised company from receiving marketplace signals in an undistorted way. If this happens over a long period, inefficiency will become endemic. But the absence of competition is not a necessary condition for nationalisation. There are examples where nationalised companies compete — and very successfully too — with private sector industry.

Proponents of nationalisation have acknowledged that competition has a positive impact within the economy. It drives efficiency, increases the search for effective operations, motivates quality improvements and encourages lower costs. The collapse of the economies of Eastern Europe and the Soviet Union have left an indelible warning as to the consequences of lack of competition. Thus nationalisations proposed by groupings such as the ANC, the SACP and Cosatu, are not geared toward command economies, but planned market economies. By the same token it is felt that state monopolies should be avoided where possible and state enterprises should compete with one another.

Slovo believes 'a competitive market which enables different enterprises to have incentives of increasing productivity, improving quality and pushing the uneconomic enterprises out of the reckoning is vital to a socialist economy.'[2]

Questions again remain: How much regulation of market forces is too little or too much? And does nationalisation inherently stop, or at least distort, the messages the market mechanism sends to the enterprise?

Risks and politics

Governments are, by definition, averse to risk. Given the responsibility of the government to its constituency, calculations of investment decisions would tend to err on the side of caution, limiting its ability to make high-risk, long-term investments. This would impact severely on industries such as gold mining where high risk is coupled with huge capital outlays.

But some governments have shown themselves more than willing to undertake long-term, and risky, investments. As Finance Minister Barend du Plessis said: 'The South African government has... over a lengthy period, established certain public enterprises which at the time were regarded as of strategic importance *or which the private sector were unwilling to accept the risk.*'[3]

It is arguable that governments can make more balanced investment decisions because there is a longer-term horizon for return. In advanced market economies (such as the USA) there is increasing criticism of the role of risk-averse shareholders who hamper management's ability to plan in the longer term.

Management requires a distinct set of priorities and goals from those of government. Management of public enterprises is said to have little freedom to take decisions in the interests of the firm. Politics, it is feared, will intervene in the decision-making process, particularly around wage policies and when cutting jobs to restore profitability. Obeying the demands of the state, rather than the needs of the enterprise, will also result in little innovation and bureaucratic management. But this 'hampering of management' is one of the reasons *for* nationalisation, not to slow down production but to develop a more participative management style.

Politicised decisions *are* likely in nationalised industries. But this will not introduce totally different considerations and dynamics into management. Management at present is partly a process of balancing demands of consumers, shareholders, employees, and others. With nationalisation this balance of power among stakeholders will shift in favour of workers and the state, depending on the process of transition outlined earlier. These power blocs would not necessarily 'politicise' the enterprise to make stakeholder management impossible; nor would powerful stakeholders necessarily make demands detrimental to the firm.

And it would not inevitably follow that government would intervene directly in management, turning managers into bureaucrats. But the warning must be heeded. The goal of running a firm for the collective good, balancing interests and making profit, however noble, is difficult to attain.

So how much government intervention should there be in the nationalised enterprise? How much autonomy for the management to act in the interests of the enterprise itself?

Those opposing nationalisation also argue that management — the key to company success — will not be properly paid and motivated. Management could, however, be incentivised by the state. In the period of transition from an apartheid economy to a mixed economy this would have to be the case — simply to prevent the flight of skills. Packages can be linked to the effectiveness of the company, meeting targets, attainment of efficiencies. As Slovo puts it, 'We are living whether we like it or not in a humanity which is moulded and driven by material incentives — both management and labour. If we disregard that we are going to suffer.'[4]

The extent to which these standard criticisms of nationalisation are being incorporated and adapted to create a new vision within the pro-nationalisation camp is significant. It is that inefficiency in nationalised industry is not inevitable; rather it is the way nationalisations have been carried out — without democracy and response to market forces — that have resulted in these inefficiencies.

NATIONALISATION IS FEASIBLE IN SOUTH AFRICA, IF

... aims are clearly defined and measurable

The aims of nationalisation must be elaborated and more clearly defined. The ANC, SACP and Cosatu have articulated these aims from the point of view of the needs of their members, and as organisations in opposition to the apartheid government. Their pronouncements are highly politicised, with nationalisation presented as a potential cure to the political and economic legacy of apartheid. The qualification that it is a complicated and difficult strategy is missing.

Proponents of nationalisation should articulate their aims *as if they were already the government*. This will alter the way nationalisation is seen, the terms in which it is put across, and make the stated aims more comprehensive and measurable. The expectations of nationalisation will become far more realistic. What the future governors also need to consider is how nationalisation will benefit companies themselves. This approach would go some way to achieving a better balance between economics and politics and between the national goals and company benefits.

If the emphasis remains on political achievements, it will be difficult to implement nationalisation. The process will cause much conflict, and whether it works or not will be a question of political opinion. And, because the focus of the exercise will be political, the health of companies themselves may not be a central concern.

... if planning is careful and detailed

The debate should be taken beyond the realm of the theoretical, into the specific. Nationalising key sectors of the economy is a high risk strategy. If the state does not utilise target companies to their full potential, key sectors of the economy will be under-utilised and the impact will be felt on growth, employment, long-term competitiveness in world markets — indeed, throughout the economy.

Targeting companies for nationalisation must be systematic, and thus should result in a more strategic set of targets than, say, the Freedom Charter, offers. Increased clarity as to the purpose and potential goals of the nationalisation is essential. It will ensure that any nationalisations will be part of an overall economic strategy, and not an isolated do-or-die reaction to a problem.

Nationalisation should be planned in full detail in advance — from the aims to the measurements of performance and the relationship between the enterprise and the state appointment of the chief executive. Only once these details are finalised should there be a move to nationalise. Nationalisation is not an abstract issue of principle, a rhetorical game. It is a delicate economic tool and must not be wielded like a sledgehammer.

... if nationalisation is not too expensive

Large-scale nationalisations — such as those envisaged under the Freedom Charter — are too expensive to finance, no matter the valuation techniques used. Nationalisation is affordable only under limited circumstances:

- Where compensation is based on declared tax value, or variations thereon. It would be prohibitively expensive to nationalise on the basis of full market value;
- Where payment is favourable to the government — such as in low-yield, tiered, non-negotiable bonds, coupled with deferred payments such as management contracts, marketing and technical agreements;
- Where there is some capacity to finance payments out of company revenues.

For the rest the government would have to support the purchase. In this event there is an opportunity cost. It then becomes a question of public opinion — is the nationalisation worth the cost?

... if the transition is well managed with management co-operation and appropriate controls

The optimum conditions for nationalisation do not exist in South Africa: Instant solutions to massive socio-economic problems are needed; the economy is unhealthy and unbalanced; there is government instability; the nation is divided on nationalisation and broader economic priorities.

Management of the transition is fundamental, from the moment when purchase negotiations begin to restructuring of the company under new owners. A key area of uncertainty is whether owners would be prepared to negotiate nationalisation. If they are, valuation and form of payment must be negotiated as well. If owners refuse to talk, classic or partial nationalisation is the second-best option.

Whether nationalisation can be implemented depends on whether the skills base exists in the enterprise. If so, nationalisation success depends on the response of existing managers, or whether they can be replaced with others with the necessary competence. If existing managers refuse to co-operate, the government can draw on politically supportive managers, some expatriates, contract managers and others. Staffing demands of nationalised enterprise, as well as a new government, will probably exceed the numbers available from these sources. Thus, nationalisation depends to some degree upon existing management co-operation. The terms on which the nationalisation takes place is crucial to finding a support base amongst this group for a future government.

Once the government has assumed ownership, it will be tempted to centralise control in the hands of politicians and government functionaries. If one thing only has been learned from Eastern Europe it is that this temptation should be resisted.

The fundamentals of state enterprise should be put in place — a commitment to running the company efficiently and effectively with clear measurement of performance, minimum politicisation, and a commitment to maximising the benefit of, and responsiveness to, market forces. As with private enterprise the nationalised company will require a workable strategic plan.

Reorganisation of the company or sector should incorporate marginalised groups — such as workers and consumers — into the decision-making process in a fashion which strengthens the company. Management's ability to act in the interests of the firm should be protected.

... if the limits are understood

The limitations of nationalisation as an economic tool should be well understood. Some of these have already been spelled out:

● It generates conflict between different interest groups in the society;
● It results in conflict between the government and the enterprise;
● Some disciplines of the market are limited, no matter what the commitment to market forces responsiveness is. For example, the threat of bankruptcy is limited, as is the threat of being taken over if full efficiencies from the assets are not attained;
● Restructuring aims merely to simulate market forces which disappear when the nationalised industry is a monopoly;
● Nationalisation cannot promise large-scale redistribution, at least not for some time. Many company resources will be taken up in payments to cover the purchase. To the extent that redistribution can take place within the firm, it will only be the product of increased efficiencies, higher labour productivity and more effective operation.

... if unexplored factors are not fundamental

There is evidence which has not been considered in this book and which may impact upon its conclusion. Most important is the risk that companies would not operate effectively under state control. The areas of nationalised industries is also beyond the scope of this book. Until these issues are fully investigated questions remain about the certainty of the success of any nationalisation programme.

This said, the concept of nationalisation *is* internally coherent. Its aims can be balanced and made appropriate to South Africa. Correct targets can be identified. Appropriate methods of nationalisation can be adopted. The target companies can be valued, and their owners compensated. Nationalisation can be financed by diverse sources and is affordable. Companies can be restructured to improve upon existing methods of work. Nationalisation can stand up to criticism.

The major qualifications outlined above cannot be wished away. To address each one will require careful strategy, implementation and management, co-operation and joint planning from all stakeholders. If these issues are not confronted head-on, nationalisation is unwise. If they are, nationalisation is feasible.

It is all a question of balance.

NOTES

1. Interview with Joe Slovo, see Appendix 1.
2. Interview with Joe Slovo, see Appendix 1.
3. *Business Day*, 21/2/90 (Emphasis added).
4. Interview with Joe Slovo, see Appendix 1.

APPENDIX 1

Interview with Joe Slovo, general secretary of the South African Communist Party (SACP)

What do you understand by the term nationalisation?
The SACP has rejected the prescription of nationalisation as part of the programme of the party. We did so because on balance it was a much abused and overused cliche, which meant different things to different people. In old thinking it connoted the transfer of legal ownership from private hands to the state. We rejected that as the kind of dispensation which results in basic transformation in the interests of the people, on its own. We opted instead for the process of socialisation which may or may not involve the transfer of legal ownership in whole or in part of enterprises during the post-transformation period.

What do you mean by socialisation?
Socialisation involves some form of participation and control by the actual producers.

What about ownership?
I don't think the question of legal ownership is the key factor, even within capitalism. The people who actually run and control enterprises — medium or larger ones anyway — are not the owners. The ownership question befuddles the issue.

Within a limited range I see nationalisation in some areas as state empowerment to participate in the direction of the sector. So the difference between the existing situation and progressive nationalisation (not the abstract one) is for the state to engage in the economy in a way which empowers it to give direction to it, in the interests of a different kind of constituency to the one which it responds to today.

How do you socialise?
It means getting worker participation at enterprise level, by which I don't mean to say that an economic project can be governed by a show of hands day-to-day on its management and direction. But actual participation through the organised structures of the producers — trade unions — and the consumers — the consumers' organisations outside the direct point of production. These people must be involved beyond the market in seeing how things should be produced, and so on.

How does the state direct production without changing legal ownership?
It does not do so in a commandist way, which is what went wrong in the commandist countries. It does it in co-operation with trade unions and so on, and by insisting on a style

of management at enterprise level which gives the workers certain participatory rights — not necessarily profit rights — consistent with the need to have hierarchies of management and decision-making processes. I am not advocating anarchy.

When most people talk about nationalisation they mean the state takes control of private enterprises to make it part of the state sector. Is that still part of socialisation?

Yes. It becomes part of the state sector. Nationalisation is the transfer of legal ownership to the state — that is all I understand by that term. That is why I do not think it is adequate, or the answer. Where you have nationalised, if it is justified — and it is not always justified at any given moment — then you have to go beyond that transfer of legal ownership and ensure that you get participation.

Even the transfer of legal ownership can be limited — we are not talking about the total transfer of ownership to the state. You could have forms of nationalisation where private capital participates — for example, the Zambian copper mines. So it does not have to involve the total transfer of legal ownership. Where the state has ultimate control — even though it is not the sole controller but has majority control, or has regulations to make it the controller — it must do so in the interests of moving towards socialisation, which is moving towards producer participation, and wider participation within these enterprises.

Can you have control without ownership?

The state could pass a law to give control without ownership — it can just do it. It can say the state has the right to take the following decisions in Anglo American. You can have regulations and legislation like that, without ownership.

Obviously the state exercises regulations over the whole economy; and by law it can provide prescriptions interfering directly or indirectly with production — like this state has done. The problem I have is that we are always looking for one prescription — nationalisation or no nationalisation. There are mixed forms. Which is why nationalisation in itself is a counter-productive word. It means so many things at so many levels — some negative — so I prefer not to use the word at all.

How would you identify a company, or a sector, which is to be socialised?

There are certain key sectors of our socio-economic formation which have to be addressed from the point of view of state direction. There are two extremes we can talk about:

* the one in the direction of non-socialisation: the small and medium sectors of the economy, non-monopolies
* the other extreme is the overweening power of giant monopolies like Anglo American. How do you deal with that? I am not advocating you nationalise 44 Main Street, with or without compensation. But you certainly have to take steps to break that overweening power. This is not a particularly socialist option. This motivation lies behind anti-Trust legislation throughout the West.

That is the one thing. You have to ensure there is not a state within a state. Then you have to examine what sort of state intervention would ensure two imperatives:

1. the prevention of an economic breakdown in a sector,
2. ensuring that the surplus which is generated in the sector is equitably distributed.

The latter you could do by taxation?

Yes. You could and would do it by taxation. But there are other elements involved. Because of the enormous power wielded by such a corporation over a huge proportion of the workforce and its lives, it is not sufficient to address only the question of how you are going to milk the cow. Here my element of socialisation comes in — you also have to ensure that the producers begin to have a stake at the point of production... This is not necessarily shareholding. In situations like that a shareholding would not be positive. You must give certain rights to create a situation in which management cannot be exercised in a tyrannical and dictatorial fashion and there is participation in relation to how the enterprise is run from the organised representatives of producers.

There is nothing necessarily challenging in that to present-day management. Some management I have interviewed — even in Anglo — are very keen on the German model.

Production Councils. No, this is not the kind of model I am talking about. I am talking about something that would give real power to the workers, even if ownership remains partly or majorly in existing hands. The state can either by legislation force a private company to give certain rights to the workers, which I do not think is the way to do it; or it can through having an economic interest in the enterprise impose itself in the direction we are talking about. The state would get involved in the enterprise by getting a stake in the enterprise which would give it certain rights — of ownership — which it would use to achieve the kind of socialism I am talking about.

So the state would participate in certain broad decision-making structures?

Yes, which could be a minority stake or golden shares.

What would then be your aim?

I would look for improving the conditions of the workforce consistent with economic viability — that is the purpose of it. Beginning to, in an affirmative way, elevate those who have been deprived of the chance of participating at higher management levels, even at the cost of a little bit of efficiency.

Would you see that in the gold mines?

Yes, on a limited scale. You could not have a gold industry consisting of 600 000 managers.

Would the state initiate this process through getting a stake in the enterprises?

Not on its own. If it is a people's state it would not do it as a state bureaucracy. It would give the trade unions an institutionalised position to act in respect of this empowerment. But it would use its ownership position as clout to ensure that this is carried out. There is no formula for this.

What do you think management response would be?

I don't think they should resist this. It will be in the interests of the country and will act to everyone's benefit. But that is not really an answer. People who are in command resent their command being interfered with in any way. They would probably resist it.

You would still need them — could you reassure them in any way?
The degree to which you can move in this direction depends on the borderline between giving employers, since they are not charitable institutions, some kind of conviction that they have security, and will get return on their investment; and assuring that the process of empowerment takes off. There is a delicate balance. The post-apartheid state would have to be conscious of this balance — they are both imperatives.

Would you say that the profit-motive is still a fundamental driving force in running these socialised enterprises? And would you criticise that?
It's a reality, I don't think there is any other. I don't think we can criticise it within the parameters of capitalism. There might be some philanthropists here and there, but by and large as a class there is only one incentive which is maximum possible profit.

Would the new state also want profit?
Yes. It would want a return for the purpose of engaging in the social sector of housing, education and so on.

Would generating a surplus be the primary motive of the enterprise?
Of course. It must be a key aim of all enterprises to generate a surplus. Except in those rare areas where, for social reasons, the state goes in for complete subsidisation — like education and even certain commodities, like bread.

How would you measure that — when subsidising transport, for example? And would you look at the welfare cost?
You have to look at a package — for example the workers' income and the distance people have to commute. You can't expect workers who for reasons of race have been shoved an enormous distance away from work (and might carry on doing so for a while until things can be reordered) — to pay economic rates. And yes, one would look at the welfare cost.

Would there be spending on worker welfare, health and safety, at the point of production?
Yes. It is a question of degree, but the requirements of health and safety at the workplace are the predominant considerations and therefore you cannot balance one cost against the other. But if the only way in which an enterprise can make profits is at the expense of the health and safety of the whole workforce, then it does not merit existence.

What about gold mining, a crucial commodity on which the country depends for exports?
You must risk a reduction of dividends and state earnings from taxation in the interest of taking reasonable precautions.

So, in every respect, workers are the key constituency to benefit from socialisation?
Yes. As far as we are concerned they are the key constituency. But they must produce, be part of the whole process of growth. They have to produce income for themselves, but also for society. Therefore there is a balance.

There is a limit, or a trade-off here. In Yugoslavia the model allowed workers to keep a large share of profits, so workers grew richer than everyone else.
You have to take that into account. If some workers are more productive than others, then they are entitled to more.

How do you measure that? It appears to be very difficult, given differing degrees of industry development, intensities of capital and so on.
Then that must be taken into account. If workers are working in conditions with obstacles to productivity then it is not their fault. This could be averaged out. It is theoretically possible. So there is a fair return for labour which does not depend upon those things over which the worker does not have control.

Would you measure management the same way?
I think so. Again I am not sure how to quantify it. But management should have similar material incentives related to productivity.

The way it works now is that managements are given performance targets for the company. If they are exceeded they get a bonus of some form or another.
I have no problems about that. We are living whether we like it or not in a humanity which is moulded and driven by material incentives — both management and labour. If we disregard that we are going to suffer. You can't have an egalitarian approach at a point in time when there are insufficient resources to give everyone a utopian existence.

Given that compromise with those ideals, there may be another one. Management says if you do nationalise they will leave the company, particularly if they are earning less and have less management control. Would you make some short-term compromises with management — in not touching salaries, for instance?
Obviously, if there is going to be some kind of redressing of economic imbalances in relation to income and wealth, some people who earn and own large amounts would find it whittled away a little bit in the long term. There would not be an immediate impact because it would be suicidal to things which would result in an immediate exodus of management skills. Perhaps as time goes on and we can develop more skills and there might be competitive possibilities between the new and the old we might not be prisoners, which we are now, of those who have had the advantage of the past — of acquiring those skills.

Are managers not using those skills to guarantee themselves large salaries — and also to stop any nationalisation programme?
There is a limit. We are going to have to accept that we are going to lose some people, and we are going to have to find ways of filling the gaps. You need to be reasoned about the degree to which you suddenly enter the new phase. There is going to be a relatively long time when you need the skills of these people, and therefore you have to try and retain them. Despite that, even for psychological or political reasons, a lot of them will go. They will also go because they will think that this socialisation I've been talking about is the

thin end of the wedge and will reach the point where they will be pushed out altogether, and so on. It is not going to be a simple process, we just have to try and minimise the degree of dislocation.

So you see a transition period where whites, and managers in particular control the wealth and power. But through state intervention there will be a gradual change in that balance of power, with the state and workers participating more and more in decision-making.
Yes. More so the workers.

What role do you think consumers who are also members of the working class, the unemployed and others will play?
Consumers must obviously play a role, whether it is under capitalism or socialism, where there is a market, at the market level. That is why I believe in the market mechanism. One of the failures of the socialist economies has been the absence of the market mechanism.

What ought to be encouraged is consumer federations which do not let the manufacturers — be they state or private — get away with shoddy products, exploiting the consumer, or which act against the end of competitiveness.

Can you elaborate on the role of the market?
The market is probably the most effective mechanism of achieving an economic surplus. The market is the process of exchange. Whether you can realise your surplus or not on the market is not dependent on any state regulation, except in certain limited circumstances, but on whether the purchaser wants your product, and whether you are producing at economic rates. This can only be determined when the exchange takes place, on the market. What has gone wrong in the socialist economies is the elimination of the market as a mechanism for realising the surplus, involving the complete move away from the market as a determinant, for example, of productivity, the economic levels needed to make an enterprise viable. These you cannot test within your enterprise, but only when your product is sold on the market. A market, or a competitive market which enables different enterprises to have incentives of increasing productivity, improving quality and pushing the uneconomic enterprises out of the reckoning is vital to a socialist economy.

I do not think the market is a fair or effective mechanism for distributing or apportioning the surplus. You have to have non-market mechanisms for that, although there is some connection between the two.

I favor, even in a state enterprise in a mixed economy, that there should be fair competition between a state enterprise and private enterprise, without state intervention at the market level.

What if there are monopolies?
There shouldn't be.

Even in the state sector?
Even in the state sector. Within a state sector, say textiles, the different enterprises have got to exchange their products on an economic basis on the market. If they can't do so then

they must go to the wall. They must not be shored up by state subsidies to maintain their low productivity in relation to others.

There seems to me to be a tension in what you are saying between, on the one hand catering for the interests of the workers; and on the other saying there are certain yardsticks which have to be used — such as productivity, profitability, efficiency and effectiveness — which will determine whether that company survives?
There is a tension. If you give workers a chance for participation, for a harmonious relationship between management and workers, and they cannot make it, should they continue? Is that the tension you mean?

Partly. You might have company 'a' which allocates retained earnings to wage improvements, future investments and so on. Company 'b' comes along and says to the workers: accept a lower wage increase and let us reinvest more in production and productivity and we'll beat company 'a'. In other words they will play a game with the redistribution side and the market force side of your model.
At that macro level you will have to have formulae to stop that kind of outcome.

Is that not interfering with the market?
No. You are not interfering with the market, but with the factory. You perhaps would say to the one factory that it is not justified to do what you said. It is a question.

But this is part of the process of competition?
In the end, though, workers would not be prepared to take a cut and lower standards compared to the others. I do not think in reality that would become an obstacle.

The key obstacle posed by a competitive economy would be the constant drive to reduce prices while increasing quality.
You could deal with this by minimum wage legislation, minimum increases and with bonuses for productivity so that there would not be this egalitarianism that deadens everything. You have this in some economies.

What about companies that are struggling. Would minimum wage increases not perhaps be the final straw for them?
You might have to make allowances for exceptions. You cannot look at this in relation to single enterprises. I might have given the impression that there should be no state intervention at all at market level. That is an exaggerated approach. There would have to be a degree of non-market mechanisms to meet the negative outcomes you have raised. But by and large it has got to be the market mechanism which has to be a test.

There seems to be a tension here between an egalitarian ideal where people put in a minimum standard and the ideal of efficiency via competition and the market mechanism?
I am against the idea that self-exploitation is OK. There must be limit to the number of hours people work. It would be improper for a people's state to allow enterprises for

whatever reason to engage in production in a way which is dangerous to the health, well-being, and leisure-life of the worker. There must be a limit to self-exploitation.

What interventions from the state would be acceptable in the company?
Where the product is so socially significant, the state has to play the primary role in determining the exchange rate for the product — like bread and other staples. That has to be subsidised and cannot be left to market forces.

The state has to play a role in determining the quantity of surplus which it appropriates for distribution — through taxes, and through its own investments.

What about capital intensity?
Where you have a social problem such as you have in South Africa of five or six million unemployed one has to balance the need for rising productivity and international competitiveness against the need to provide employment for people, which if you don't would collapse the whole social system. How you approach that balance is a question. A phase of labour-intensive production — even though it might disadvantage you in export — could begin to generate this multiplier effect. There is no recipe.

What are your aims of nationalisation? What do you want to get out of it?
I want to get out of it a society in which the producers have a sense of participation and not alienation from the products which they produce. I think that is more important than it signifies just in relation to the day-to-day functioning of a factory — it is a completely new concept of the way people relate to their society. From that can be born a more integrated community and moving towards greater equity and egalitarianism.

Mandela focuses on redistribution. Cosatu focuses mainly on workers control. Do you focus primarily on ideological aims?
It is also a combination of redistribution of wealth, give the state the power to upgrade conditions for disadvantaged people, participation of workers, moving towards socialisation. It is not just based on some idealistic ideological objective.

What do you see as the importance of growth?
Without growth everything is meaningless. If socialisation does not achieve it then there is no justification for it. But I believe it will achieve it. When the producer begins to have a real stake in what he is producing and in society as a whole then I believe we will achieve greater growth and greater productivity. But I am not really concerned with growth as a thing in itself. We had the ideal growth rate in South Africa between 1960 and 1976, but there was no redistribution, the gap between white and black increased, there was repression and so forth. But you cannot redistribute wealth which is not there, but the wealth growing does not imply fair redistribution. You need both.

APPENDIX 2

Interview with Kennedy Maxwell, past-president of the Chamber of Mines

What do you understand by the term 'nationalisation'?
Taking over by the state of the control of an industry or corporation, with or without payment.

Is this the kind of acquisition being thought of at the moment?
Some kind of payment has been mentioned. But I can't see how they can afford to pay for it. Where do they get the money from?

Would bonds be an option?
That presupposes that nationalisation works and that there will be some form of pay-back. I believe it would not work and there will be no pay-back.

Why?
Because people who are not accountable to private shareholders, but are accountable to the state, which ostensibly has a bottomless pit of funds, are not incentivised and not nearly as determined to work to achieve profits as people in private enterprise are. So you lack the incentive for productivity and the determination to achieve. If you read about the history of nationalised companies, they all sooner or later leaned on the state to keep themselves alive.

Whereas the gold mines, for example, have not done that?
As you know in the past there has been some intervention from the state to keep the marginal mines going. The current view of the state is that they do not wish to bail out marginal mines. I believe that is right. While there are 15-18 marginal mines, many of them will be forced to close, with all that means for the loss of jobs and exports. The fact is that we are fighting like crazy to try and stay afloat.

Would this not be the same under nationalisation?
No, I don't think so. Under nationalisation they would buckle much sooner, and they would say they have to keep the jobs and the revenue going. It has happened in the rest of Africa and overseas. The state says we cannot do without these things.

Do you think it is possible for the state to incentivise?
If you had asked me last year I would have said no. It would appear that SATS are beginning to introduce some incentives into their operation. However, I feel they knew that there was a fall-back position all the time. Now, given that they have been told they have to survive on their own, there is going to be a loss of jobs. The people who keep the jobs will be trained up, become more effective and if we can keep a profitable transport network going, that in itself will create more jobs elsewhere.

Do you think it is ever justifiable to run a loss-making enterprise, like education or the post office?
In principle no. But in practice probably yes in certain circumstances. But where there are certain circumstances where the state should run things at a loss that should be very clearly identified and explained to parliament with all the figures then revealed so that one knows the cost of that.

Why are people advocating nationalisation in your opinion? Who are the players?
They simply believe it is a mechanism to redistribute wealth. The players are the unions and the ANC. I question the degree to which the ANC is really committed to the policy of nationalisation. I believe the ANC believes it has to redistribute wealth in order to establish its credibility in society.

So you think it is a negotiating position — take a hard line, and let go of it slowly in exchange for something else? And what if they are serious?
That is my perception. Then we have some serious discussions to do. I firmly believe that in order to redistribute wealth you have to try and increase the size of the economic cake. SA is not a wealthy country. We have been hammered by sanctions. And we have to recoup that and all the jobs it cost us. So we have to try and stimulate the economy about 5% or 6% per annum if we are going to provide the jobs that we want. So my first criteria for trying to get a more equitable distribution of wealth is providing jobs which requires increasing the rate of growth of the economy which in turn requires greater investment in the country. If we are going to attract greater investment then we have to show them that we have viable propositions to invest in.

Everyone agrees on growth and job creation and investment. But it is advocated that in addition, nationalisation is needed.
They must believe that they can run the industries better, or as well as, private enterprise and that they would then redistribute the profits that arise.

So you think redistribution is the crux of the call?
What else could there be?

Worker control — access to industrial democracy?
I can see that they believe they would achieve industrial democracy. But, in practice, I really question whether the nationalised companies would be more democratic than private

enterprise. I don't want to be too general there, but if you look at South Africa there have been more introductions of democratic practices in privatised companies than in state controlled organisations. I think Eskom has started to become more democratic, but that is because they have started privatising. But there has been more initiative towards democratisation in private enterprise than in state enterprise.

Given the kind of state we are dealing with?
Yes ... But even if you look at the rest of Africa they are army-type organisations.

There has also been the argument that nationalisation would give greater access to decisions about capital investment.
Private enterprise has certain criteria about decisions relating to capital investment. What would the state do differently? We have seen the government of yesteryear go for Mossgas! If you had given private enterprise R6-billion years ago and asked what they would have done with it, they would have suggested rather a project like the following: electrify every region of South Africa and give every individual electricity. There would have been a multiplier effect — demand for cookers, TVs etc. It was a political decision to go for Mossgas.

Does that always have to be the case? Is it inevitable?
I think the state always believes it has a cause which is good for political reasons — they are politicians.

Even if there is a complete transformation of the current state — and democracy is introduced?
The people who administer the state will be politicians. Politicians do not make decisions based on profit and those sorts of criteria. It is true of Mangope, it is true of every politician I know.

Not a great example ... what about the argument that nationalising the commanding heights will give greater ability to plan the economy to improve growth, make us competitive on the world market, etc?
I immediately ask: which planned economy in the world has ever worked? You can rationalise and say that if you allow a total free market economy you will have distortions. But at the end of the day, whatever its flaws, a free market economy will grow faster and stronger than a planned economy.

Under a free market economy is there room for nationalised services and products?
I suppose that it would be necessary to provide a centralised health care system, and thereby need to nationalise health. I would hope that it would be a clearly structured insurance health scheme rather than the type of scheme set up in Britain, which is exploited by the masses and also the rich, which provided disincentives for doctors and did not provide the services it set out to do.

Any others?
I would tend to exclude transport, but recognise that around certain cities mass transport for commuters would be something that should be looked at by the region. For the rest transport should be privately run. Electricity supply ... a country as small as South Africa warrants having a central supply, which would not leave it open for instituting competition. Therefore you should leave it under one umbrella under the state. But I am not satisfied that would be the best system. I would think you could establish competition. But if you couldn't then you would have to have some very meaningful representation from the consumers on the council. Eskom does provide some representation on the Board of the consumer. But I am not sure whether they are providing the kind of service they should be to control the whole financial structure of Eskom.

Bringing in the example of consumers brings in the argument about responding to market forces. if you were able to simulate that in your structures where nationalised industries were accountable to consumers, is it a more workable form of nationalisation?
If you had to have nationalisation, then I would say yes.

What about other representation, such as workers?
I firmly believe in participative management and have introduced it into the gold mines we run (at JCI). So I would go along with that 100% as a form of management whatever the nature of the organisation was. If you were to say that workers should come in and sit in the Board, then I would not object to that so long as you structure the functions properly. If they were to sit on the Board and were presented with globular figures, just as if the Board was answerable to parliament, then those MPs would not be able to get into the nitty-gritty of the operation and point to which assumptions for the budget are relevant or irrelevant. It is difficult to pass judgments from outside. You need some skills and detailed understanding to take meaningful decisions.

You were talking earlier about this 'fall-back' position where managers of nationalised industries could just draw on this immense pool of resources from the state. What if there were strict limitations on finance?
I come back to the fact that politicians will always make decisions relative to the votes they think those would get or where they believe that their philosophies and policies are right, regardless of cost.

And if you limited the power of politicians to do that? By making nationalised industries responsible to consumers, workers, the public at large, rather than just parliament alone? An example could be the Tennessee Valley Authority.
They are also competing with other utilities as well. So they are not subject to a monopolistic situation.

So you must then introduce the element of competition?
It is vital. And you would have to make a carte blanche decision that if the competition is better than you are, either you do something about it or you go out of business.

So you think that nationalisation is more a danger when you have a monopoly in a sector and it is accountable only to government?
Yes.

Is this not the conventional wisdom of what nationalisation is — a monopoly accountable to the government?
Maybe that is the way people think. But then I would like to see examples of where it has been done successfully elsewhere. The Coal Board in Britain, the steel industry went down the tubes with the best will in the world believing that they were running those organisations competitively.

How do you explain those failures?
There was not the incentive on the part of the people who ran these organisations... we will cut jobs, or we will cut expenditures or we will do something in order to retain our competitive position. They were protected by the state, they could fall back on the state, they could prevent imports, and so on.

If you are going to lose your business because you can't match the competition, that is an enormous incentive to stay alive. If you remunerate skilled people at competitive rates within that corporation and not within a state hierarchy of job levels, then the person will decide: am I going to make more money out of doing something smart or am I just going to sit back and let the company go down the tubes, and he will then set out to incentivise to get the maximum share out of the profits.

What do you think of NUM's demand to nationalise the gold mines?
I feel it is misguided. I really don't believe the NUM or the future government of the country will be able to run the mines any better than we do. That is not to say that we are perfect. There is a lot of scope to try and do a lot better. But with the shortage of skills we have already in the country, I can't see that we will do any better with nationalisation — because we will lose a lot of the skills.

Why would people leave?
I really believe people would just leave. They would find a better job somewhere else.

Even if salaries, perks and everything remained the same?
Given time they would, because if you are responsible to specific people who have got very clear deadlines and are prepared to make decisions on the hard financial issues, they will stay. But if you have politicians stepping in and saying: 'no you cannot lay off 10 000 people here, keep the company going', then the rot sets in and it just spreads like a cancer.

You have mentioned firings quite a few times ...
I am sorry if I am giving the emphasis that productivity can only be achieved by laying off workers. That is not true. Very often with participative management you can say to your employees: 'fellows, this section is going to make a loss, what shall we together do

about it?'. It may be that managers and employees all agree — and I know of cases of this — that they should all take a ten percent cut, or increase productivity.

At the end of the day my philosophy is that companies should try to remain profitable and increase productivity. If that means fewer people do the same amount of work, or fewer people doing an increased amount of work, then it will generate, through the multiplier effect, more business throughout the economy. You will then get more jobs and more work available. Ultimately politicians will stop that process from unfolding.

If nationalisation was to happen, with payment, what would the response within different levels of managers in the mining industry be?
The smart managers would leave the industry fairly soon. The less smart managers would stay. Therefore the level of productivity and the smart decisions would start to diminish, and then you would be back into your political scenario. In Zambia the smart people left and the copper mines just went downhill. The revenues which the state expected to get to repay the bonds just never materialised.

Does that not become a self-fulfilling prophecy if the best managers leave and things go sour? If they stayed, then there may be a chance of success.
It becomes an issue of 'from each according to their ability to each according to their needs'. If you had altruistic managers who would give their all for the sake of the needy, then maybe it would work. But it is in the nature of man that if he were not remunerated for his work, but was simply doing it for the needy, then his attitude changes. If he sees that he is being remunerated for his hard work, and his survival depends on keeping the company going, which in turn depends on keeping all employees motivated, then that would bring about proper remuneration and incentive.

But that could continue ... for example, if targets are set for growth and you keep paying managers saying: 'reach those targets and we will reward you for it'.
I suppose you can do that. Your shareholders are now the state. Now you want to expand production because you can achieve more. Is your money going to come from the state?

Either the state or debt financing because there is no share market...
Let us take the mines. To open a new mine at the end of the day will cost R3-billion. I won't get a return on that for nine years. It is risk business. Would the state want to invest in something like that? I doubt it. Why would they?

Because it will create jobs? Because we need growth?
Yes. But you want the money to run the state. It is less likely to go for that long-term risk business. We have to go for a fair share of that capital overseas. To attract the overseas investor he needs to know that his investment is not going to be nationalised. Look what happened to the share market the minute nationalisation was mentioned. The stock market collapsed.

The bottom line that you have to address is whether the benevolent dictator that you see running the country or the nationalised industry is going to continue being the benevolent dictator, or whether the position of power and lots of bribes is not going to turn him around so that he becomes as bad as the rest. Your bottom line is: where has it ever worked elsewhere?

The Tennessee Valley Authority in America?
There it was operating in a competitive environment, and it had customers on the board...

Local nationalised industries like Iscor, which is why it is being privatised?
Yes. But it was only when Iscor started to be privatised and they looked at how they would satisfy the private sector that it started to get smart.

That is what you have to inject to shake things up a bit — smart management...
You are getting to the right ingredients for running businesses. It is my belief that in the nature of man and in the nature of politics that nationalisation does not work.

Can any scale savings be made from nationalising the gold mines?
We already have combined research and development, labour training, and so on. The Chamber of Mines provides a lot of those services. There is constant debate about what would be better — centralised efforts or individualised decentralised efforts. The net result is identifying common areas where it is better to have centralised efforts. Others — like trackless mining — we went for ourselves because no-one else wanted to. So there is no real savings or scale gain from nationalisation.

Given that there are so many demands for nationalisation, do you think it could be stopped?
Yes. I think one has to argue the thing through. I think private enterprise has to recognise the very real needs of the masses, and the fact that there is homelessness and there is a total distortion of the education system, and so on, and therein lies the very problem of trying to get the economy to grow and trying to bring non-racialism into the business on a full-scale basis. We have to consider how we are going to try to bring an improvement in wealth distribution. Wages you can tinker with — but whether you put them up a few percent is not really going to make a difference. But if we all share in the profits by making the company and the economy bigger — that could achieve a wealth distribution. You can achieve that by a direct share in the profits from quarter to quarter, share in capital and equity and allowing it to grow. Certainly I think private enterprise has got to address the problem of homelessness and education to the extent that it can, with the government.

Is the General Mining scenario an option — where Anglo hands over a portion of itself to people like it did to Federale Volks to create General Mining?
One would love to see that happening again. The distinction is that by then you had a group of Afrikaners who had built up Federale and who had a level of expertise so that they were able to pick up the ball and run with it. Unfortunately, because of the education and training system of the past, I don't think there is a group of black people who could pick up the ball and run with it. I would love to see it happen.

APPENDIX 3

1. Possible measurement devices of aims of nationalisation

AIM	POSSIBLE MEASUREMENT DEVICES
Ideological	
The new socialism	Subjective opinion. No objective criteria.
Mixed economies	Subjective, mostly. Also growth and distribution patterns, level of conflict in society.
Political	
Industrial democracy	Mainly subjective. Also changes in board structures, degree of consultation with workers
Shifting decision making to a group responsible to the public	Mainly subjective. Also setting up of public controls. Actual nationalisations, new structures
To achieve national self-determination	Withering away of white domintion of economic and political life, while not being replaced by another power structure. Mainly subjective yardsticks.
Correcting racial imbalances	Access of different races to the vote, the key centers of power, institutions of learning, the distribution of wealth and access to resources, and others.Subjective considerations in choice, measurement and conclusions reached.
Control over monopoly power	Existence of monopolies. Ability of their controllers to take decisions unilaterally. Mainly subjective yardstick.
Re-nationalisation	Objective measurement - numbers of privatised industries re-nationalised
Restoring the Land to its rightful owners	Objective measurements available are land redistribution, returning removed communities to their land, and others. However, many of the decisions preceding the act are subjective.

APPENDIX

AIM	POSSIBLE MEASUREMENT DEVICES
Economic	
Redistribution of wealth (incomes)	Income distribution patterns, measured over a long period.
Redistribution of wealth (services)	Availability of service to differing groups defined by race, income, gender, age and others; as well as patterns of use.
Correcting failures of the market mechanism	Change in wealth distribution patterns, decrease in statistics indicating market failure. Development of a balanced economy. Some objective criteria, many subjective judgments
Filling an investment gap	New projects undertaken by the state in new investment areas.
Preserving, creating employment	Objective measurement available: jobs saved and created through nationalisation.
Increasing productivity	Productivity measurements showing totally new patterns of behaviour.
Changing employment practices	Subjective, but measurable.
To assist economic planning by the state	Improvements in economic life by state interventions. Difficult to measure.
Stabilisational and macro-economic objectives	Adaptability of the economy. New research and development from the state sector, balanced economic development. Change in economic dictators. But mostly subjective.
AIMS NOT INCLUDED IN SA	
'Natural monopolies'	Easy to judge.
Structural efficiencies	Change in key performance indicators.
Response to economic crisis, or profitability crisis	Numbers of firms requesting to be nationalised
Cost-benefit optimisation	Cost-benefit calculations. Still a new 'science'.
Economies of scale	Objective measurements. Also can measure experience curve benefits if appropriate.
Developing the value chain	Objective measurements: new industries integrated, new projects begun (eg beneficiation)
As a response to international developments in the industry/global competitiveness	Not difficult to measure.Comparative statistics on performance such as innovations, productivity, price, quality. Improvements in competitiveness on the world markets..

2. Timing, forms and source of compensation and potential effects

Timing	Form of payment	Source of payment	Potential effects
Immediate	Cash - local currency -	Government printer, already circulating, tax revenue,	Inflationary, Inflationary Opportunity cost,
		Debt - government or company Public donations	Inflationary, Burden, Cash drain, Domestic savings,
	foreign currency	Government reserves	Exchange rate, Balance of payments
Deferred	Bonds Dividends	Government Company	Inflationary, Burden, Cash drain
Indirect	Management contracts	Company	
	Marketing agreements	Company	Dependence
	Patent agreements	Company	

3. *Structure and value of the Rembrandt Group*

	NETT WORTH	NETT WORTH OF HOLDING OTHER THAN IN REMBRANDT
Rembrandt Trust and Rupert Family Trust	Unknown as not listed, but about R320-million (8,6% of nett worth of Rembrandt Group Ltd)	R0,00
↓ 51%		
Technical and Industrial Investments Ltd	R627-million	R0,00
↓ 60,8%		
Technical Investment Corporation Ltd	R748-million	R0,00
↓ 40,8% (from Technical Investment Corporation Ltd); 8,6%		
Rembrandt Controlling Investments Ltd	R1 842-million	R0,00
↓ 51,3%		
Rembrandt Group Ltd	R3 608-million	

(Source: Riordan, R, 'The Nationalisation of Industry in South Africa', in *Monitor*, April 1990, The Journal Of Human Rights Trust, Port Elizabeth.)

4. Major companies controlled by Rembrandt Trust

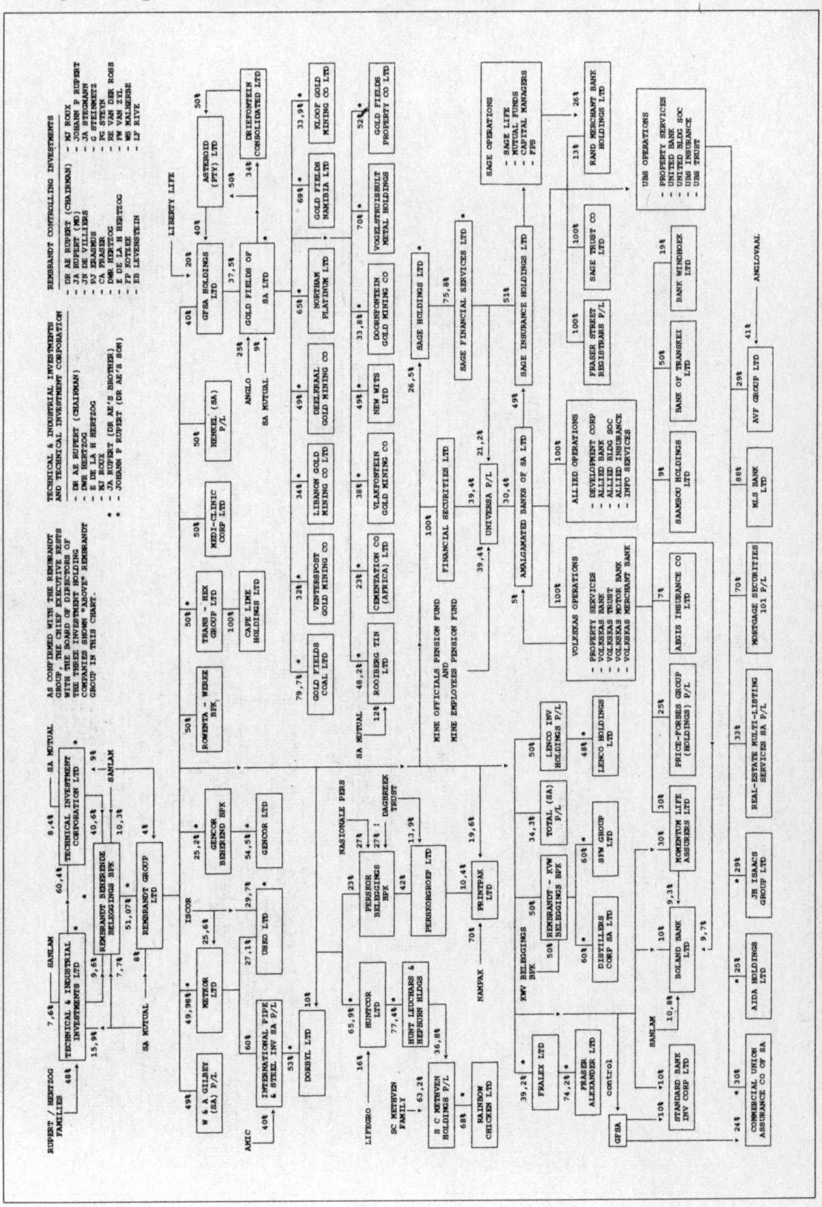

AS CONFIRMED WITH THE REMBRANDT GROUP, THE CHIEF EXECUTIVE RESTS WITH THE BOARD OF DIRECTORS OF THE THREE INVESTMENT HOLDING COMPANIES SHOWN "ABOVE" REMBRANDT GROUP IN THIS CHART.

TECHNICAL & INDUSTRIAL INVESTMENTS AND TECHNICAL INVESTMENT CORPORATION

- DR AE RUPERT (CHAIRMAN)
- DWR HERTZOG
- E DE LA H HERTZOG
- MJ ROUX
- * - JA RUPERT (DR AE'S BROTHER)
- * - JOHANN P RUPERT (DR AE'S SON)

REMBRANDT CONTROLLING INVESTMENTS

- DR AE RUPERT (CHAIRMAN)
- JA RUPERT (MD)
- JN DE VILLIERS
- PJ ERASMUS
- CA FRASER
- DWR HERTZOG
- E DE LA H HERTZOG
- FP KOTZEE
- EB LEVENSTEIN
- MJ ROUX
- JOHANN P RUPERT
- JA STEGMANN
- G STEINMETZ
- PG STEYN
- RE VAN DER ROSS
- FW VAN ZYL
- WS MALHERBE
- LF RIVE

RUPERT / HERTZOG FAMILIES
SANLAM
SA MUTUAL
TECHNICAL & INDUSTRIAL INVESTMENTS LTD
TECHNICAL INVESTMENT CORPORATION LTD
REMBRANDT BEHERENDE BELEGGINGS BPK
REMBRANDT GROUP LTD
W & A GILBEY (SA) P/L
METKOR LTD
ISCOR
GENCOR BEHEREND BPK
ROWENTA - WERKE BPK
TRANS - HEX GROUP LTD
CAPE LIME HOLDINGS LTD
MEDI-CLINIC CORP LTD
HENKEL (SA) P/L
LIBERTY LIFE
GFSA HOLDINGS LTD
ASTEROID (PTY) LTD
ANGLO
GOLD FIELDS OF SA LTD
DRIEFONTEIN CONSOLIDATED LTD
AMIC
INTERNATIONAL PIPE & STEEL INV SA P/L
USKO LTD
GENCOR LTD
DORBYL LTD
GOLD FIELDS COAL LTD
VENTERSPOST GOLD MINING CO
LIBANON GOLD MINING CO LTD
DEELKRAAL GOLD MINING CO
NORTHAM PLATINUM LTD
GOLD FIELDS NAMIBIA LTD
KLOOF GOLD MINING CO LTD
ROOIBERG TIN LTD
CEMENTATION CO (AFRICA) LTD
VLAKFONTEIN GOLD MINING CO
NEW WITS LTD
DOORNFONTEIN GOLD MINING CO
VOGELSTRUISBULT METAL HOLDINGS
GOLD FIELDS PROPERTY CO LTD
LIFEGRO
HUNTCOR LTD
NASIONALE PERS
PERSKOR BELEGGINGS BPK
DAGBREEK TRUST
SC METHVEN FAMILY
HUNT LEUCHARS & HEPBURN HLDGS
PERSKORGROEP LTD
S C METHVEN HOLDINGS P/L
RAINBOW CHICKEN LTD
NAMPAK
PRINTPAK LTD
MINE OFFICIALS PENSION FUND AND MINE EMPLOYEES PENSION FUND
SAGE HOLDINGS LTD
FINANCIAL SECURITIES LTD
SAGE FINANCIAL SERVICES LTD
UNIVERSA P/L
SAGE OPERATIONS
- SAGE LIFE
- MUTUAL FUNDS
- CAPITAL MANAGERS
- FPS
FRALEX LTD
KWV BELEGGINGS BPK
REMBRANDT - KVW BELEGGINGS BPK
TOTAL (SA) P/L
LENCO INV HOLDINGS P/L
AMALGAMATED BANKS OF SA LTD
SAGE INSURANCE HOLDINGS LTD
FRASER ALEXANDER LTD
DISTILLERS CORP SA LTD
SFW GROUP LTD
LENCO HOLDINGS LTD
VOLKSKAS OPERATIONS
- PROPERTY SERVICES
- VOLKSKAS BANK
- VOLKSKAS TRUST
- VOLKSKAS MOTOR BANK
- VOLKSKAS MERCHANT BANK
ALLIED OPERATIONS
- DEVELOPMENT CORP
- ALLIED BANK
- ALLIED BLDG SOC
- ALLIED INSURANCE
- INFO SERVICES
FRASER STREET REGISTRARS P/L
SAGE TRUST CO LTD
RAND MERCHANT BANK HOLDINGS LTD
GFSA
control
UBS OPERATIONS
- PROPERTY SERVICES
- UNITED BANK
- UNITED BLDG SOC
- UBS INSURANCE
- UBS TRUST
STANDARD BANK INV CORP LTD
BOLAND BANK LTD
MOMENTUM LIFE ASSURERS LTD
PRICE-FORBES GROUP (HOLDINGS) P/L
AEGIS INSURANCE CO LTD
SAAMBOU HOLDINGS LTD
BANK OF TRANSKEI LTD
BANK WINDHOEK LTD
COMMERCIAL UNION ASSURANCE CO OF SA
AIDA HOLDINGS LTD
JH ISAACS GROUP LTD
REAL-ESTATE MULTI-LISTING SERVICES SA P/L
MORTGAGE SECURITIES 101 P/L
MLS BANK LTD
AVF GROUP LTD
ANGLOVAAL

Reproduced with permission from McGregors on-line information Pty (Ltd)

5. Major operating subsidiaries of the Anglo American Corporation

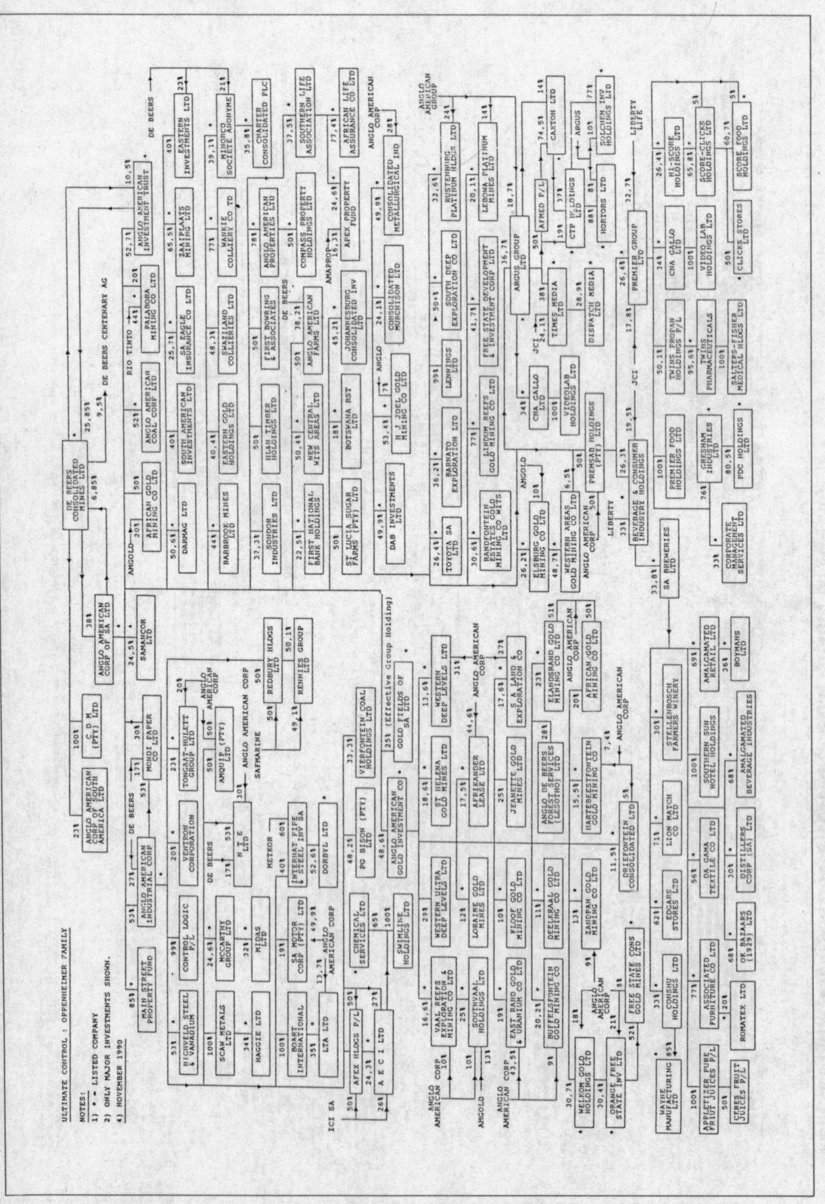

Reproduced with permission from McGregors on-line information Pty (Ltd)

6. Major interests of SA Mutual

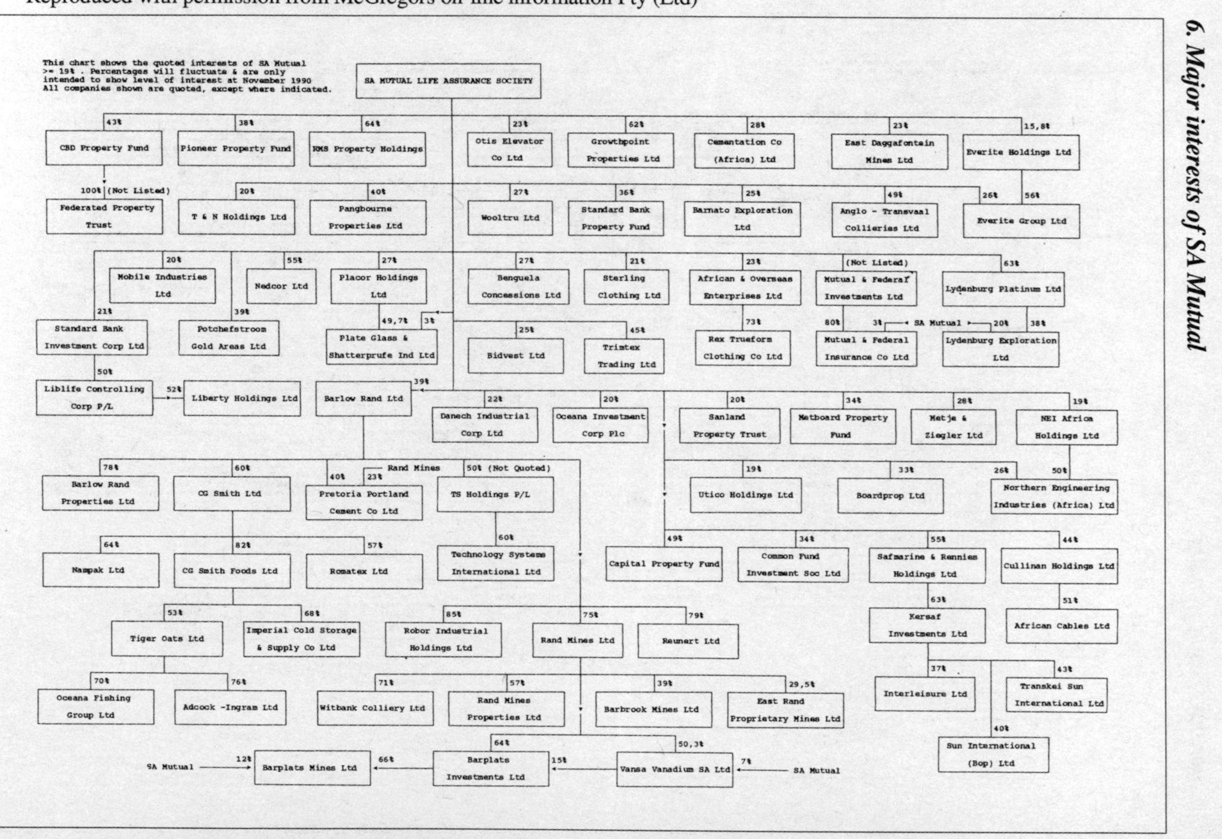

7. Major interests of Sanlam

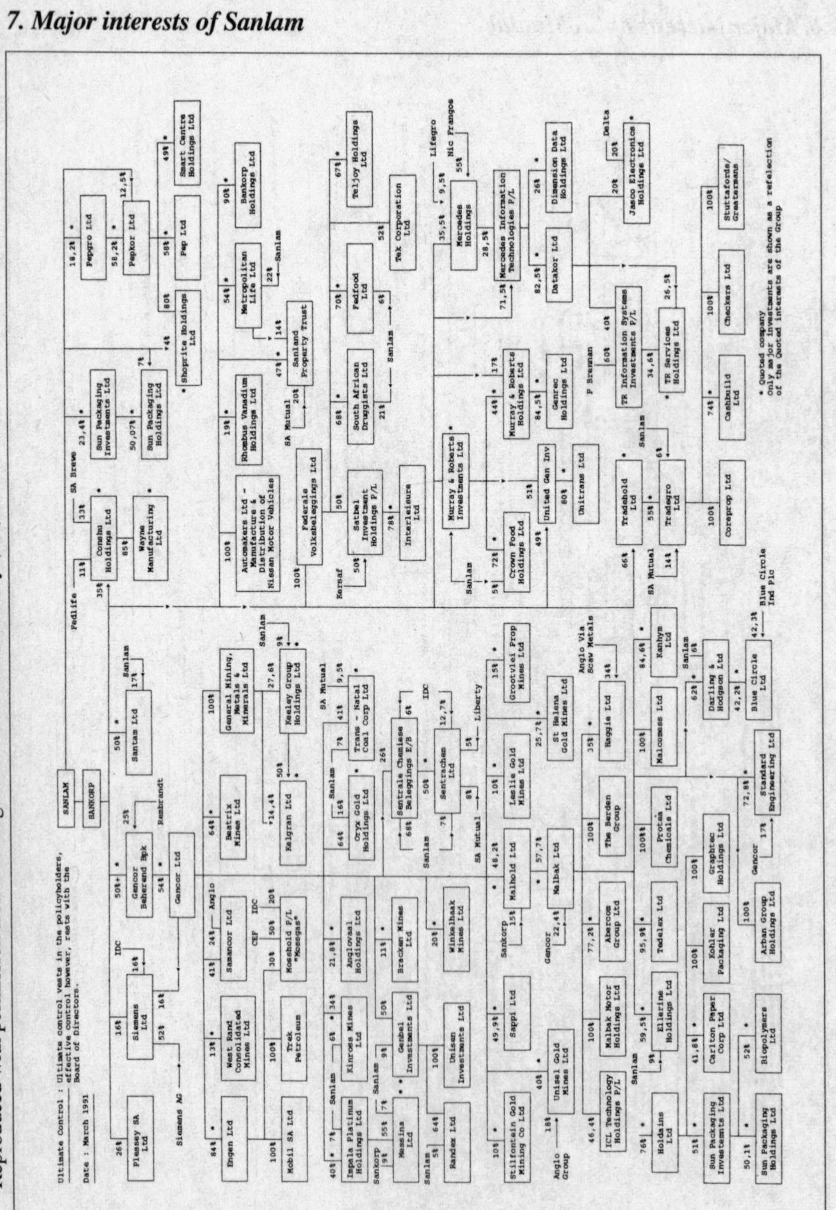

Reproduced with permission from McGregors on-line information Pty (Ltd)

8. Size of bond dividend payments could cover at different interest rates

Sector/company	Annual payment	Interest rate	Bond size
Chamber of Mines	R2 200 m	16 %	R13 800 m
		14 %	R15 700 m
		12 %	R18 300 m
Anglo American Industrial Corporation	R 239m	16 %	R 1 500 m
		14 %	R 1 700 m
		12 %	R 2 000 m
Barlow Rand	R 570m	16 %	R 3 600 m
		14 %	R 4 100 m
		12 %	R 4 800 m
Amgold	R 275 m	16 %	R1 700 m
		14 %	R2 000 m
		12 %	R2 300 m
Rembrandt	R 104 m	16 %	R 650 m
		14 %	R 750 m
		12 %	R 900 m
JCI	R 160 m	16 %	R1 000 m
		14 %	R1 100 m
		12 %	R1 300 m

9. Possible responses to different nationalisations

Type of nationalisation	Scale	Conflict generated	Likely response
Confiscation	Large	V High	Capital flight, JSE Collapse, Brain Drain (Large)
Confiscation	Small	High	Capital Flight, JSE (Large Drop), Brain Drain (Medium)
Classic (unfair)	Large	High	Capital Flight, JSE (large drop), Brain Drain (Large)
Classic (unfair)	Small	High	Capital Flight, JSE (large drop), Brain Drain (Medium)
Classic (fair)	Large	High	Capital Flight (Medium), JSE (small effect) Brain Drain (Medium)
Classic (fair)	Small	Low	Capital Flight (small), JSE (small effect), Brain Drain (small)
Negotiated	Large	Low	Capital Flight (small), JSE (small effect) Brain Drain (small)
Negotiated	Small	Low	Capital Flight (minimal) JSE (minimal) Brain Drain (minimal)

INDEX

A

B

D

E

F

G

H

I

J

L

M

N

R

S

T

V

W

Z

This book was indexed by Sharon Rubin
of SM RUBIN INDEXING SERVICES, Johannesburg